What a
Modern Catholic
Believes About

THE RIGHT TO LIFE

by Richard Westley

the thomas more press
chicago illinois

ISBN 0-88347-029-2

To my wife

Ethel

*Whose virtue and faith have revealed to me
a world I might never have known existed*

Contents

AN UNALIENABLE RIGHT–REVISITED

A S Americans and Catholics we cannot enter into a discussion of the "right to life" unfettered by our traditions. No matter how much some might like to think that we can start discussing this problem free of presuppositions, our life in society is part of a continuum. This is just another way of saying that some sort of continuity with the past is one of the prerequisites of every social order. Regardless of what position we adopt, it will be the stance of men and women formed and shaped by a political and religious atmosphere in which life was once held to be most precious and inviolate.

Our Declaration of Independence clearly states: "We hold these truths to be self-evident, that all men are created equal, that they are endowed by their Creator with certain unalienable Rights, that among these are Life, Liberty and the pursuit of Happiness." It is difficult to imagine how the matter could be put more forcefully. Not only does each man possess the "right to life" but that right is "unalienable," not depending on the will of his fellows but coming directly from the Creator. And all this is said to be beyond doubt or dispute because it is self-evident. Even the most perfunctory and cursory acquaintance with the contemporary scene leads one immediately to ask how what was once self-evident could have suddenly become both widely unrecognized and hotly disputed.

The stance of the Catholic church has been no less definite. The vigor with which the church has consistently fought for the inviolable "right to life" has been established beyond question by contemporary scholars. In accord with that tradition, Vatican II reaffirms that: "From the moment of conception life must be guarded with the greatest care. . . . Whatever is opposed to life itself, such as any type of murder, genocide, abortion, euthanasia, or willful self-destruction are all infamies." Yet while the official church remains steadfast, who among us is not aware of the current disputes going on among Catholics on all these points?

Obviously the American Catholic of today confronts his world profoundly affected by the ideals of his church and his country. This does not mean that each Catholic in the United States merely parrots Vatican II or the framers of the Declaration of Independence. Some do, but many do not. Of those that do not, some would alter the traditional stance only slightly, while others would so profoundly alter the American attitude toward the "right to life" that it would change the kind of society we are asking one another to live in. But even these people are affected by the past, at least to the degree that they must take some pains to separate themselves from it. It is unrealistic and possibly pathological for us to deny our heritage and attempt to proceed as if it never existed. Even if we are anxious to move beyond the values of our past, it is more intelligent and realistic to accept them as that which determines the context of the present growth, and as something with which we do have some continuity whether we like it or not. It is not insignificant that for American Catholics to be in touch with their religious and political past, means to encounter a vital and living respect for human life and its equivalents.

One consequence of this heritage is that we have not yet moved to the point at which life is no longer a value of any sort. As a people, we remain *totally* unaccepting of willful murder and genocide. As a people, we are *generally* opposed to suicide (except in those cases where it can be identified as euthanasia). There is a growing opposition from our people to a "war of interest" as opposed to a genuine "war of self-defense," and capital punishment is no longer accepted as inevitable. All of which is a striking indication that we are a people nurtured in a profound respect for life, and that our heritage still exercises some real influence on our present values.

If the current situation differs from the past, it is in the fact that as a people we are less willing to accept an unreflecting application of our cultural and religious values to concrete cases. After the amazing spectacle of the Nuremberg trials in which men claimed immunity from prosecution because they simply did what they were told, that is, they blindly applied the values of their culture to concrete cases, contemporary man has come to the conclusion that no value, no matter how noble, no matter how rational, ought to be adopted by individuals without critical reflection. No man has the right to simply abdicate his conscience in favor of the values of his country or of his church. Should he nonetheless do it, he cannot expect his fellows to relieve him of responsibility for his actions. If there is anything to be learned from World War II, it is that.

And so it was almost inevitable that in our day Americans would refuse to guide their conduct by the simple rubric "unalienable right to life," and would insist on retaining the right and power to discern in the concrete situations of life when, where and how this rule ought to be applied. As was to have been expected, once the questioning of the meaning of this traditional value began, we found that we disagreed about the application of the "right to life" principle in the two special cases of abortion and euthanasia. That is one reason why we find a "right to life" debate currently raging in those two areas.

Of course, there are other reasons as well. Medical technology advanced to the point where the transplantation of vital organs became more than science fiction. But if 20th-century man was to move forward in this area, he had to find a way of procuring transplantable organs which would be medically, biologically, socially and culturally acceptable. Finding suitable donors was always a major problem, but once found an equally serious problem remained. When is it appropriate, in a society overtly committed to the unalienable right of each to life, to take an organ from the donor?

If one had to wait until the donor was dead according to accepted medical practices (absence of vital life signs like heartbeat, respiration and response to certain stimuli), very often the organ desired would no longer be fit for transplantation. To overcome this impasse, a new definition of "death" was essential. In the wake of transplantation experimentation the one hammered out was the absence of a normal human brain scan. Elaborate machines were invented to sustain the other vital life signs in persons who had suffered irreversible "brain death." Doctors were able to sustain respiration, blood circulation, heartbeat, and cleansing of the blood for indefinite periods. The much debated question became—Is one who evidences these vital life signs with the help of machines really alive? Are such procedures really sustaining the life of a man, or are they merely sustaining some vital life signs in a corpse? The very fact that advances in medical technology have made such a question possible indicates that there are important difficulties with a simplistic recourse to traditional "right to life" thinking about the terminally ill and euthanasia.

Medical advances on the other end of the life cycle have also been instrumental in precipitating difficult "right to life" questions. Modern obstetrics has established beyond all doubt that at no time is the fetus "part of the mother" or merely "maternal tissue." Though the old wives' tale remains widespread, it is no longer scientifically respectable to consider the child in the womb to be a mere organic adjunct of the mother.

Once scientifically established, the biological difference and distinctness of mother and fetus gave rise to a new medical specialty aimed at safeguarding, healing and promoting life in the womb. It is called fetology. Transfusions, surgery, and a wide range of diagnostic tests and therapeutic procedures have all been performed on intrauterine fetuses. This marshaling of medical knowledge and skill in behalf of the life of the yet unborn has not always proved beneficial to them. Though fetology principally aims at promoting the life of the unborn, it obviously cannot control the use to which the knowledge it supplies is put, and sometimes that knowledge has been used against the life in the womb.

The significant point for us in all this is that the diagnostic expertise of fetology allows parents to determine very early in a pregnancy whether the life they have begotten is flawed or malformed, and it opens the possibility of their doing something about it. Of course, their options run in two diametrically opposed directions. They may embark on a program which brings all the advances of fetology to bear on the fetus in an effort to correct or arrest the problem. Or they may choose to simply abort the fetus. For many, the second option is no longer out of the question because of improved techniques of early abortion, and because of the growing opinion that fetal life especially in the first two months is not really "human." Such a stance clearly breaks with our traditional commitment to the "right to life" and has added to the pressures for a change in our understanding of it. Medical progress (on the levels of transplantation, life support systems, fetology and abortion) has also been a real factor in furthering the current controversy.

If our new sense of freedom with its wider range of possible responses and the unbelievable advances in medicine can be cited as prerequisites which made the current "right to life" debate possible, they are not sufficient to explain the sense of urgency with which that debate has been conducted since 1965. To account for that aspect of the situation, one has to take note of the insertion into the public forum the highly volatile issues of overpopulation and ecology.

The language of that aspect of the "right to life" debate was not value free; it was charged with high emotion as terms like "population explosion" and "the population bomb" were introduced into our everyday vocabulary. Nothing less than the survival of the species on the planet was at stake. The "ecological clock" had been running down and according to the best estimates of the experts we had about thirty-five years to turn the process around or we were inevitably doomed to extinction. The burgeoning numbers of people on earth threatened the "quality of life" of all of us. Nature and evolution had mechanisms which controlled the populations of the other species on earth; only human reproduction was increasing unchecked. This fact led Sir Julian Huxley to exclaim: "Unless he chooses to mend his reproductive ways, man is heading for the greatest disaster in his history." It all boils down to one insistent and ever recurring question for Huxley: Do we want more people at a lower level of existence and a higher risk of disaster or fewer people at higher levels of existence with more opportunities for fulfillment?

While population plays an important role in determining the quality of human life, it is by no means the deciding one. It is not so much a question of how many people live on earth as it is a question of *how* the many people there live. Highly industrial populations, even when smaller than larger agrarian ones, cause greater harm (imbalance) to the environment because of their increased consumption and the problem of the disposal of industrial wastes. A child born into an industrial society is not only another mouth to feed, his lifestyle requires that he consume more of the precious resources of the earth than his counterpart in an underdeveloped country. To maintain the high quality of life found in contemporary industrial societies, not only must reproduction to be curbed; in addition, an educational program must be begun to alter the way our people look upon children.

Once seen as a boon and blessing, children must be viewed more realistically as a threat to our survival and as potential polluters of the environment. As we Americans have more and more adopted this view, it was only natural that we would re-examine what many feel is an indiscriminate, naive and absolute commitment to life. The outlawing of abortion, and the allocation of precious medical resources to the terminally ill must be viewed in the context of overpopulation and the demands of environmental economy. From that vantage point they can no longer be taken for granted as beyond the proper boundaries of intelligent debate, nor should those who choose to debate these issues be considered un-American.

One Approach

Much more could be said about the various factors which have promoted a re-evaluation of the "right to life" in our day. Hopefully enough has been said to indicate that the issue is by no means a simple one, and that there is at least the possibility of having rational men on both sides of the argument. After all, the fact that one man disagrees with another on this issue does not necessarily mean that the stance of the other is an irrational one. Disagreement, at its best, is itself a product of reason and hence quite rational. That means that eventually the ultimate question will become: When rational men disagree on the understanding of the "right to life" in this culture, how should the issue be resolved? Of course, one way to avoid having to ask yourself this difficult question is to simply dismiss your opposition as irrational. That tactic has been employed on both sides of the "right to life" debate, without notable success. Having learned something from that experience, I shall avoid such name calling and try to work toward some sort of answer to the ultimate question.

To that end, I have chosen to limit my consideration of the "right to life" to those two areas which have become so problematical recently: abortion and euthanasia. The limitations of space have prevented my considering other important facets of the "right to life" such as war and capital punishment. Each of these would itself require a whole book. It is perhaps worth mentioning that I do not feel that the problem of contraception falls directly into any "right to life" category. We will be dealing only with life already conceived, and conceived life only in its most vulnerable phases, i.e., in the womb and on the brink of death.

I have divided the presentation into two parts. The first part is concerned with what a modern Catholic "thinks" about the right to life. However, I should warn the reader that he will not easily find what I think on the matter in the first three chapters. They are devoted primarily to describing the "right to life" debate, and to presenting some of the arguments on both sides of the question. I did not allow myself the luxury of speaking entirely in my own name until chapter four. The second part consists of only one chapter and it is concerned with what a modern Catholic "believes" about the right to life. There I have tried to see if faith and our commitment to Christ can cast any additional light on the subject and give some indication of how a Catholic imbued with the new theology might want to answer the ultimate question.

Those who pick up this book already having some familiarity with the abortion and euthanasia debates might want to go directly to chapters four and five. Doing so is not without some risk, however, because the positions taken there are intelligible only if one has become somewhat convinced of the futility of those debates.

When all is said and done, I claim no special authority for what I say. Each author in this series simply shares with his fellows what is in his own mind and heart on provocative topics. The proper response to such sharing is dialogue, not rebuttal or condemnation. In any case, what follows is simply what *this* modern Catholic thinks and believes about the "right to life."

Part One

WHAT A MODERN CATHOLIC
THINKS ABOUT
THE RIGHT TO LIFE

Chapter One

CHOREOGRAPHING THE DEBATE

IN choosing to call the public discussion of the right to life a "debate," I am *not* using that word in some broad sense simply to indicate that there are two sides to the story. Nor is my use of the word "debate" merely descriptive; I fully intend it to be a value judgment of a pejorative sort. The word comes from the same root as "combat," which is appropriate because a debate has all the attributes of a "battle" (which incidentally is another word from that same root). If the current right to life discussion is a debate, it would be dishonest to describe it as a search for truth, or to suggest that it is an open-minded discussion having the characteristics of authentic dialogue. Indeed, one calls the discussion a "debate" precisely to affirm that it has little or nothing to do with truth, and to deny that it is in any real way dialogical. Put succinctly, one is *partner to* a dialogue, but a *partisan in* a debate.

Do you remember the members of your high school debating

team? They were the ones who walked the halls with their little boxes filled with three by five index cards from which, on a moment's notice, they could produce facts, statistics and arguments of various degrees of cogency, both pro and con, on the given debate topic of the year. Do you recall the Kennedy-Nixon debates? From such simple experiences as these we can characterize a debate as follows: A debate is an adversary proceedings, pro and con, in which one is under no obligation to really hold the position he defends. It is a kind of theatrical performance aimed at persuading an audience or a third party who passes judgment on the proceedings which are so programmed in advance to avoid surprises that they can almost be staged and choreographed. Finally, a debate is aggressive, self-justifying and defensive.

Sometimes men set out to have a debate right from the start, but at other times they inadvertently end up in one because they fall short of their original goal—human communication. In that case, debate is what happens to abortive attempts at dialogue. Unlike a debate, dialogue is not an adversary proceedings; it aims at overcoming division by achieving a unity which is the result of the shared risk of openness and mutual vulnerability. Because authenticity is the hallmark of every genuine dialogue, it precludes role-playing and the theatrics of scoring points or winning favor. Dialogue seeks an interpersonal relationship with the other whereby he is himself affirmed and becomes for me the occasion of new growth, insight and revelation. Dialogue thrives on the unexpected, and its outcome is always risk-filled and uncertain.[1] Finally, dialogue is marked by so profound an honesty, that it is not only not defensive but even self-incriminating if necessary.[2]

A superficial acquaintance with the right to life discussions in the literature gives one sufficient evidence for concluding that it is a debate not a dialogue. All minds are made up, there is no attempt made to speak *to* the other side only *against* it. Each side presents arguments which are known in advance by the other side, which always comes up with appropriate counterarguments. No assertion is made without its being challenged, no question is raised which does not immediately elicit a negating response from the opposition. After a while, as you read the literature you find you can predict with a high degree of accuracy what will be said and which tactics will be employed. Only rarely do you find a new and creative presentation, but even when you do, before long it too generates its own proper response from the opposition, and both items are thereafter included in the accepted choreography of the discussion. The dance becomes longer and more intricate, but it can never end. It is in the nature of a debate on values and freely chosen perspectives that once started it go on endlessly. And so it has. Indeed, so it must. The expert, in that case, is not the one who can bring the debate to a successful conclusion, for that is impossible. He is, rather, the one who masters its ever more complex choreography.[3]

While it is true that the right to life debate is no dialogue, this does not mean that the two sides share no common ground. Even an argument requires that there be a common context within which one may take either a positive or negative stance. Without such a taken-for-granted context, discussion itself becomes impossible and one is left with two parallel monologues which never meet or intersect.

Common Assumptions

Despite the heated opposition between the partisans of this debate, their common ground is quite considerable. They share common assumptions and methods. (Some have gone so far as to suggest that they even share one and the same argument; it is just that it is pointed in diametrically opposed directions.[4]) Anyone wishing to enter the right to life debate with the expectation of being understood must accommodate himself to this common context which includes the acceptance of: (A) a pluralistic society; (B) certain medico-biological, sociological and legal facts; (C) the ideal of rationality; and (D) the contemporary emphasis on individual will acts as the focal point of morality.

A. *Accommodating to Pluralism.* An important aspect of our history as a nation has been the high tolerance we show for dissent and a variety of value systems.[5] Life in the United States, and therefore discussion as well, takes place within a context of pluralism. Yet a pluralistic society cannot achieve an unmitigated pluralism. Society is required to exhibit at least the minimum unanimity of a shared conviction to tolerate diversity. Absolute pluralism is a contradiction in terms for any viable social institution. Nonetheless, a mitigated pluralism is not only possible but highly desirable in order to protect the inviolability of individual human conscience.

But if the sacredness of individual conscience is writ large in our history, a consequence of that sacredness is no less important. The obligation to form a right conscience and to follow its dictates falls on the individual, not on his fellows (except when they too are considered as individuals). The obligation which does fall on them is that they respect the conscience of another without qualification when it is right, and with certain qualifications even when it is wrong. This is just another way of saying that they must be guided by their own consciences when evaluating whether the conscience of another is right or wrong. From this perspective, pluralism is not only possible and desirable, for in the light of the basic principle of the autonomy of human conscience it becomes obligatory. Of course, we are not obliged to be *actually* divided from one another on basic values, but we *are* obliged to leave that possibility open.

As a basic principle of our republic this theoretical commitment to pluralism is rarely, if ever, challenged. In practice, however, Americans have the same difficulties with dissent and diversity as do the other members of the human species, which shows that we are far less noble than our principles. In our individual lives we would crush the discord and dissent from conscientious objectors, women's liberationists, and others. We make no secret of how we feel privately about those whose consciences are opposed to our own. Yet should we move into the public forum, we feel reluctant to implement our private feelings by imposing our conscience on others. This is one of the prerequisites for admission to the public forum in our society. We retain the right to disagree, to debate, to persuade, and to work for our private values, but when in the public forum we forego the expression of opinions or the performance of acts which would undermine the right of others to oppose us there. Those who violate this canon of accepted practice are either denied access to the public forum or are no longer taken seriously when they do speak there.

Since the right to life discussion is a debate, and since a debate aims at persuading in the public forum, it is not surprising that all the parties to the right to life debate tacitly accept the challenge of accommodating their words and behavior to the limitations of pluralism. Failure to do so would be the most effective way of insuring that they would not be listened to in this culture.[6] Well aware of this fact, both sides make strenuous efforts to fashion their arguments in strictly humanistic terms and to avoid being parochial in the public forum. By so doing, they have automatically created some common ground for their debate.

B. *Accepting the Facts.* If personal values, ideologies and religious convictions are all sensitive items in the public forum due to our commitment to pluralism, that leaves very little else with which to operate comfortably there, except the "facts." But since in an adversary proceedings the facts are not so easily come by, it is best to have independent experts, not party to the controversy, supply a common fund of "facts" for the use of both sides. For example, if you were in a hotly disputed argument about who was the greater baseball player, Micky Mantle or Babe Ruth, you might in the course of the argument disagree with your opponent about which of them had the higher lifetime batting average. Now while it makes perfect sense to debate the relative merits of Mantle and Ruth as baseball heroes, it would be ludicrous to attempt to settle the matter of the batting average by means of a debate. Ordinarily a debate does not aim at establishing a fact or group of facts, but is more often concerned with the proper evaluation and interpretation of these facts. In this case, one would go to the record book, or to one who was long acquainted with the statistics of baseball in order to settle the factual question of which of the two men had the higher batting average. Of course, that would not settle the matter since one could decide to place more or less importance on a higher lifetime batting average in his judgment of which one was the greater player. In general then, one accepts the facts as given (the data) by an independent authority in order to debate about something else, i.e., the real meaning and significance of the data.

In the right to life debate, implementation of this ideal procedure is not so simple for two reasons. First, the facts on which that debate depends cover several areas of expertise, which cannot all be mastered by one and the same person. And second, not all the so-called experts remain independent and impartial. A good number of them become partisans in the debate itself, which means that the objectivity of the entire enterprise is jeopardized. Despite these difficulties, there is still a general consensus on both sides of the argument that since the debate has occurred in the context of reforming the existing laws against abortion and euthanasia, it ought to be conducted on the basis of the generally accepted findings of the life sciences (biology and medicine), the social sciences, and the law.[7] Obviously there is no agreement on just which findings of which experts are to be taken as "the evidence" in the debate, but it is taken for granted by all that evidence from experts is essential to make any position taken in the debate a reputable one.[8]

C. *Embracing the Ideal of Rationality.* Of course, our reliance on the scientific findings of experts makes our stance, whatever it may be, more reputable because all such experts are committed to *the ideal of rationality*. Just how reputable an ideal that is in our culture can be judged from the fact that each of us feels deeply wounded if he is characterized as "irrational" by his fellows, and immediately begins to employ extreme measures to reestablish his rationality. Any debate, by definition, is an attempt by one side to present a more rational view of the matter under discussion than the other. The parties to a debate strive for rationality because they agree in advance that the greater rationality necessarily elicits support and automatically wins the debate.

The importance of rationality in human affairs can be seen in the obvious distinction we all make between giving a "reason" and giving a "motive" for an action. If you asked a man why he killed his mother-in-law, and he told you that he didn't like her because she was always nagging at him, you would no doubt thank him for sharing the "motive" for his crime with you, but you could still deny that was a sufficient "reason" for murdering her. Motives explain why a person does something; reasons justify his action. Motives cannot justify an action because all too often they are shot through with subjective passions, imaginings, fantasies and untruths. Reasons, on the other hand, are held to be objectively true, at least in the sense that any impartial and rational agent in the same circumstances would decide to act in exactly the same way. A man can justify his own actions only if he is able to convince himself and others that any man trying to be objectively honest in similar circumstances would have acted similarly.

Because the right to life debate is committed to this ideal of rationality, it can be described as a search for the justifications, pro and con, which can be discovered or produced with respect to abortion and euthanasia. To so characterize it casts some light on another dimension of the ideal of rationality. *The rational is never simply given to man.* Man discovers it through the expenditure of great effort and only then presents it to his fellows for approval in the form of a necessary movement of thought called an argument. An action is considered rational if one can discover objective and justifying reasons for doing it, reasons which can be expressed in a principled argument which embodies a necessary movement of thought. Admittedly this is a high ideal, yet all parties to the right to life debate share it and are very anxious that their arguments meet the high standard of objective rationality.

D. *Stressing the Moment of Decision and Choice.* A final working hypothesis which permeates the right to life debate (though it is not as widely held as the preceding three), is that abortion and euthanasia are primarily a matter of free choice and decision. Kings, judges and doctors may get used to making life-death decisions but the average man only rarely, if ever, is faced with one. But when he is, as in cases of abortion and euthanasia, the life in question is either of his own flesh or at least of his own family. That alone is sufficient to make his decision more "agonizing" and "terrible" than the life-death decisions of government officials or medical professionals.

In the right to life debate man is seen as faced with a decision crisis in the present. The debate aims at supplying the justifying reasons for present choices, the assumption being that men have no trouble with decisions once they have justifying reasons for their choices. No attention is paid to the obvious fact of experience that even when we know what is right we have great difficulty in doing it. Obviously there is something more to decision making than justifying reasons. All of this is ignored by the debate, which proceeds very much as if once a man understands what is right he will have little or no difficulty in doing it.

The Basic Differences

All this talk about a common set of assumptions and a shared perspective should not cause us to lose sight of the fact that there is a deep and abiding division at the heart of the right to life debate. That difference can be described as running from the most conservative principle among the anti-abortion/euthanasia group to the most liberal principle among the pro-abortion/euthanasia group—on the status of human life.

A. Anti-Abortion/Euthanasia (pro-Life[a])

I) Human life is inviolate at each and every stage of its development and no one has the right to act against it directly.

II) Human life is inviolate at each and every stage of its development, but occasionally it is permissible, though regrettable, that we act directly against it.

B. Pro-Abortion/Euthanasia (pro-Life[c])

III) The right to life is not absolute, but conditional. It is inviolate only under certain conditions. When these conditions are not met or when one's right to life conflicts with the rights of others a calculation must be made as to which right ought to prevail.

IV) In the case of abortion and euthanasia where the humanness of the life involved can be seriously questioned, the right to life is no longer a significant consideration.

Before turning to a consideration of these principles, it is important, in the interest of fairness, to come to some acceptable way of designating the two sides of this debate. Those who are dubbed as being "anti-abortion/euthanasia" are rightly upset by the use of that label. After all, they would remind us, they are not primarily against anything, they are FOR life. For convenience then let us hereafter speak of this group as the one which is for the absolute value of human life and designate them as the *pro-Life[a] group*. On the other hand, those who are said to be "pro-abortion/euthanasia" aren't too happy with that designation either. To speak of them in that way seems to indicate that they are primarily for the taking of life. Rather, they view themselves as being primarily for a certain quality of life which can most quickly be achieved, so they contend, by means of abortion and euthanasia. Since they are FOR life of a certain quality, we can designate their commitment to a certain condition of life by calling them the *pro-Life^c group*. By using these designations, which more clearly indicate what each group is primarily for, we shall avoid prejudicing the case before we present it.

The pro-Life^a group. Those who place an absolute or almost absolute value on human life and who either totally or generally exempt human life from the calculus of conflicting rights or interests belong to the pro-Life^a group, but they do not all operate from the same principle. Those who adopt Principle I do so because they feel that the direct taking of innocent human life is always unjustified. Until recent advances in medical care made it unlikely, situations did arise in which the life of an expectant mother and the life of her unborn child came into direct conflict. We did not have the medical skill to save both, and could save either one only by direct action against the other. According to Principle I, two deaths are better than one murder. That is, it is better to do nothing and allow both mother and child to die, than to take direct action against one for the sake of the other.[10]

Those of the pro-Life^a group who find Principle I too restrictive, have adopted Principle II. They judge that it is dishonest to say you are for human life, and then to advise in the life-against-life case that one must stand idly by and watch mother and child die. How can such a response to a tragic situation be said to be respectful of life? Common sense seems to indicate that if you are for life you will be sure to save at least one of them. The proponents of Principle II hold that there are regrettable occasions when one's commitment to life requires a direct action against an innocent human life.

Perhaps a case other than a prenatal one would help clarify what divides the proponents of Principles I and II. The classic case is given of the driver of a gasoline tanker who has an accident and is trapped in the cab as fire breaks out at the rear of the truck. The flames begin to spread and the heat keeps everyone away. The driver looks at the police officer keeping the crowds back and says: "Don't let me burn to death. For God's sake, shoot me!" The proponents of Principle I can't imagine the officer shooting the truck driver, while the proponents of Principle II are able to at least entertain the possibility of granting the doomed man's final request. Principle I advocates a hands-off policy at all times, while Principle II leaves open the possibility of direct intervention in certain very specific and extremely rare cases.[11]

The pro-Life^c group. A man crosses the main dividing line of the right to life debate once he gives up a commitment to innocent human life as an absolute value. As soon as one begins to question whether in the context of other rights the right to life is to be automatically invoked, he has moved over into the pro-Life^c group. If he adopts Principle III, he will be obliged to judge each and every case of the right to life in the light of the circumstances surrounding it. He will forego the convenience of claiming that life is an absolute value, and will assume the difficult task of judging each case on its own merits. Unlike the proponents of Principle II who allow but few exceptions, the proponents of Principle III open the door to a situation in which exceptions are anything but exceptional.

The proponents of Principle IV applaud the efforts of the proponents of Principle III toward liberalizing our right to life commitment, but they see no reason to burden man with the overwhelming task of constant evaluation of individual cases. Such a stance would be understandable only if the lives in question were certainly human, but in all cases of abortion and in many cases of euthanasia, this just is not the case. Therefore it is better to remove those cases from the context of the right to life debate, and to allow people total freedom to do what they want about them. Principle IV is very liberal from the point of view of the right to life debate, but it is not a libertine position of total license. It does not contend that one may adopt any position he wants with regard to every life-death decision. Principle IV would not condone infanticide, murder, and indiscriminate attacks on human life. Rather it suggests that abortion and euthanasia are special cases which do not properly fall under the right to life principle, and it is only in such cases not covered by the right to life principle that one may do as he pleases. In all other cases, the proponents of Principle IV would want to adopt one or other of the first three principles.

Summary

The right of life discussion is not a dialogue in which the partners proceed in a mutual and open-ended search for truth. It is rather a debate in which the participants are locked into an adversary proceedings which can be won by one only at the expense of the other. But a debate presupposes a common problem on which to focus, a common set of facts on which to base the arguments, as well as common assumptions which form the context within which the debate can proceed. In the right to life debate, the common problem is abortion and euthanasia, and the common facts are the findings of biology, medicine, the human sciences and the law. The common assumptions made by both sides to their own benefit are: a commitment to pluralism, a willingness to accept the findings of experts, endorsement of the ideal of objective rationality, and the focusing of the debate on the crisis-mentality of individual choices.

The partisans to the right to life debate are divided on whether innocent human life should be valued absolutely or conditionally. Each one proceeds from a principle which he chooses to adopt as the starting point for his arguments. And as we shall see, one's choice of principle profoundly effects the way he argues. In the next two chapters we shall attempt to catalog the key arguments of both sides of the abortion debate, and to present some of the elements of the euthanasia debate.

Chapter Two

CATALOGUING SOME
ABORTION ARGUMENTS

I N the days before the current abortion debate, a distinction used to be made between *feticide* and *abortion*. The former referred to the direct killing of the fetus within the womb. The latter referred to the expulsion from the womb (by force or natural causes) of an intact, nonviable fetus. Now that the precision afforded by such a distinction no longer seems important, both are spoken of as "abortion" in the broad sense, without distinction.

Those engaged in the abortion debate present two sorts of arguments. The first kind rests on some overriding principle which is taken to be self-evident and in some way acceptable to all. The argument tries to show that if you accept the principle you must also accept the position for or against abortion which logically and rationally follows from it. We shall call all such reasonings *principled arguments*. There is a second class of arguments, used by both sides, which reasons from some concrete set of consequences (usually of an unacceptable nature) which can be easily avoided if one adopts the position of the framer of the argument for or against abortion. In what follows, all such arguments will be designated as *consequential arguments*. As we might expect, the principled arguments are much stronger and persuasive than the consequential ones, because it is often possible to avoid the unacceptable consequences by a means other than the one suggested. In order to be really conclusive, a consequential argument would have to show that there is only *one* way to avoid the undesirable consequences, i.e., the suggested way. With regard to abortion this is not so easily done.

In this chapter, we shall make no attempt to get into the abortion debate as such, but will merely present some of the more cogent arguments presented by each side along with the most obvious rebuttal available to the other side. We leave it to the astute reader to decide for himself the merits of each argument, although we shall make some brief comments of our own after each exchange.

Some Pro-Life[a] Abortion Arguments

Argument No. 1—"The" argument against abortion. One of the cornerstones of any viable human society is the principle that there must be a limit to what a man can manipulate for his own interests. A man is not at liberty to do something just because he wants to or is capable of doing it, for there are limits placed on him by the fact that he is called to come to his own fullness as a man in the company of his fellows. Society is impossible in the absence of such a limit and only chaos can ensue.

The first and most important limit, because it is the foundation of all the others, is the right of others to life. According to Principle I, human life, or the life of a person, must be inviolate at each and every stage of its development. Human life wherever it occurs is sacred and cannot be reduced to a means to some other end, because it is an end in itself.

But the life which is conceived by two human persons can be nothing but human life, therefore under no condition can the life of a fetus be violated. Abortion violates the innate sacredness of human life and under no circumstances can it be justified.

Rebuttal to Argument No. 1. Granted that there are limits to what a man may manipulate for his own interests. Granted too that the fundamental limit is met when we deal with the lives of other human beings. It only follows that abortion is improper if one accepts the fact that a fetus is human life deserving of such respect from the start and at each and every moment of its development. But this is surely not the case.

Everyone knows that the use of the adjective "human" is, to say the least, ambiguous. If one were to find a bone which had been buried for a long time and wanted to know whether it was a "human" bone, he would analyze its cellular structures under a microscope. If it had the right structure and the correct number of chromosomes, it would be judged by all to be "human" in one of the legitimate uses of that word, but this would scarcely entitle it to all the privileges of a person. If this is what the framers of Argument No. 1 mean by calling the fetus "human," we agree, but fail to see how this makes their case. For a lock of hair is "human" in that same sense, and so haircuts would be ruled out along with abortions.

Perhaps the framers of Argument No. 1 are using the term "human" in another of its accepted senses, namely, that organism is considered "human" which has properly human organs present and functioning. (This would rule out a cadaver, for which the most that could be said is that it *was* human.) But this will not seem to make the case either, for obviously the fetus is "human" in this sense only some time after conception.

A third use of the term "human" applies to a fetus which is viable, that is, capable of sustaining its own life apart from its mother without extraordinary artificial means of support. Certainly such a use of the term "human" is no help at all to the framers of Argument No. 1, since this would mean that the fetus is not human until the sixth or seventh month.

Obviously, the framers of Argument No. 1 must be using the adjective "human" in some other sense. And there is a fourth use of the term which seems to suit their purposes admirably. That organism is called "human" which has the potentiality or capability of developing into a viable fetus with distinctively functioning organs composed of cells exhibiting the characteristically human structure. Now granted that this is one of the accepted uses of "human," and granted too that those who restrict the meaning of "human" to this fourth use would have to logically hold that the fetus is human from start to finish and that it is inviolate at each and every stage of its development, there seems to be no compelling reason why one must accept this restricted and narrow use of "human." The framers of Argument No. 1 have not established that their choice of the meaning of "human" is *the* only meaning it can have. Since we have shown that it has other accepted meanings, we are under no obligation to accept the conclusion of the argument.

Comment. Argument No. 1 could have been presented in several different ways. It could be called the Natural Law argument, or it could be called the traditional Catholic argument, but I have tried to give it a purely humanistic expression in keeping with the assumption that a parochial expression of the argument would violate the ground rules of the debate.

The rebuttal attempts to zero in on what is the weakest link in the argument. The rebuttal accuses the framers of the argument of arbitrarily choosing that definition of "human" which best suits their own purposes. By contrast the other side feels itself to be at liberty to choose any of the other uses of "human" which best serve its interests. The proponents of Argument No. 1 would have something to say about why they chose as they did. The discovery of the genetic code and the recognition of the importance of the genotype[1] are the scientific (biogenetic) basis for the claim that human life is a continuum and that it is impossible to designate a particular moment in development when the life in question *becomes* human. It is either human from start to finish or it will never be human at all.

Many feel that this new medical evidence settles the matter and insures that Argument No. 1 will be conclusive. I would only remind the reader that no fact, medical or otherwise, can definitively settle the right to life debate on abortion. For the debate is not over whether there is biological continuity or not, nor is it even about the proper meaning of the term "human"; but rather it is over whether the fetus represents an instance of human life of such a character as to be deserving of all the respect given to human persons. As far as I know, no biological information can settle that question.

Finally, Argument No. 1, or some variant of it, is the only principled argument against abortion. In saying that, I do not mean to imply that it is not sufficient or that there is something wrong with having only one. Quite the contrary, to have even one is no small thing. What I do want to note here is the fact that that makes all other arguments against abortion to be of the consequential type. They are usually thrown in for good measure to gain a wider acceptance of the principled argument. But if the truth be told, if Argument No. 1 is valid and true there is really no need to argue any further.[2] As an argument which aims at ruling out further argument on abortion, it has sometimes been simply called *the* argument.

Argument No. 2—An argument from legal consequences. There is a great furor brewing these days aimed at repealing or at least reforming the traditional anti-abortion laws of the various states. On the face of it, that seems simple enough, but in fact such changes strike hard against two of the basic principles of our legal system, i.e., equal protection under the law, and due process. To do away with our traditional laws then is not a simple matter at all, for it could very well weaken the foundations of the republic.[3]

Following the lead of English common law, the American courts have recognized the unborn's right to life, his right to property, and since World War II have affirmed the unborn's right of recovering for harm done due to negligent injury to his mother while she carried him. Since the law has recognized in the unborn a sovereign subject of rights, the fetus is entitled to all of the protection of the "equal-protection-before-the-law" provision of the American Constitution. To legalize abortion on demand (abortion without justifying reasons) would not only be to arbitrarily deprive the fetus of the equal protection to which he is entitled, but it would be to do so without due process. If the integrity of our legal system is to be maintained such changes would require nothing less than a Constitutional amendment.

Rebuttal to Argument No. 2. It is small wonder that the legal situation surrounding abortion is muddled. That is to be expected once the law, which should restrict itself to matters of the common good and equity in public dealings, oversteps its proper bounds and moves into the area of interpersonal relationships. The government has no business involving itself in the sexual relations of its citizens. The legal crisis is not at all over whether the fetus' rights are being upheld, but rather whether the State has the right to intervene to force parenthood on those who do not want it.

Secondly, the law is by no means immutable. Laws are the codified traditions and mores of the people. Once the people are no longer committed to the values embodied in their laws, they are at liberty to change them. Failure to do so can only precipitate a widespread disrespect for the law. What Argument No. 2 forgets is that prolonging and defending the traditional legal structures is not the only alternative open to us. We can always change them to meet the changing times. To the charge that such a change would alter the kind of society in which we live, it should be said that we certainly hope so.

Comment. In presenting Argument No. 2, I have tried to avoid getting too involved in the legal technicalities of the matter. For those the reader is referred elsewhere.[4] But it should be stressed that the legal context of the abortion argument is a very important one. Much energy has been expended on both sides, and the proponents of Argument No. 2 are tireless and self-sacrificing in their efforts to stem the tide toward more liberalized abortion laws. Yet I cannot help feeling that their efforts are by their very nature temporary and doomed to be inconclusive. The basic problem is not a legal one, and the move to shift the abortion debate into the legal forum is simply a tactic used by both sides for their own ends. The law cannot stand indefinitely against the will of the people. If the anti-abortion fight is to be won, it cannot be finally won in the courts, but will be won by tactics which inculcate a commitment to the respect for life embodied in the law.[5] This should not be taken to mean that I think the legal fight should be abandoned as useless, but rather to mean that I feel that the legal fight cannot be the only one waged by those in favor of Argument No. 2.

Argument No. 3—An argument from social consequences. Liberalized abortion brings in its wake a whole series of unacceptable social consequences, any one of which could be used as the basis for an argument of this type. For example one might argue, as Dr. Violet Anderson of the University of Aberdeen does, that readily available abortion has a detrimental effect on the sexual attitudes of young people, causing a regression toward what she has called "primitive behavior." By this, she means that they become totally self-centered, and give little consideration to the future consequences of their acts or to the rights and feelings of others. At least that was the conclusion she reached after a five-year study of the students at the University. One could also argue that the spectacle of abortion mills in New York and elsewhere are a public expression of a disrespect for life which rivals Vietnam as a national disgrace. Or finally, one might point to the fact that liberalized abortion is subverting the medical profession committing it to the destruction of life rather than to its enhancement. And it does this precisely at a time when the medical facilities of the country are no longer adequate to the task of caring for the health of the nation.

The litany could be expanded, but the argument is always the same. Liberalized abortion brings in its wake a series of effects which corrode our society in important respects. To avoid these effects, we need only resist the current pressures to liberalize our abortion policy.

Rebuttal to Argument No. 3. It is interesting that the so-called social consequences of abortion are always enumerated in this way, but surely it is evident that there are some equally unacceptable social consequences of not liberalizing our national abortion policy. Frightened young girls who become pregnant will in growing numbers seek out the services of back-street abortionists; there will be an increase in the number of unwanted children in the world; and individual freedom will be arbitrarily restricted. There will always be some evils in our society, it is just a matter of which ones you can tolerate and which ones you can't. On such matters men of good will may disagree.

That disagreement is particularly evident in the cases presented in Argument No. 3. The behavior characterized by Dr. Anderson as "primitive" may seem so to her, but others might find it liberating and acceptable. Then too, to liken the abortion enterprise in New York to Vietnam is to assume that the lives in both cases are of similar worth and dignity. But one can't assume that in this debate; that is the point at issue. If you see the New York abortionists as a national disgrace it is because you insist on thinking of the fetus as fully human, which is another point on which both sides disagree. Finally, the disagreement comes to the fore again when you see the performing of abortions as somehow contrary to the goals of the medical profession. It is possible to see the abortionist in a more positive light, as making a contribution to the health and welfare of our society. The point is simply this, what one takes to be an unacceptable social consequence, another judges to be an asset and a sign of progress.

Comment. As the exchange indicates, the arguments from social consequences are a very mixed bag indeed. The two sides in the debate all too often don't meet one another in the context of such arguments, because they do not agree from the start on what constitutes an unacceptable social consequence. But even when they do agree on that, they seem to get themselves bogged down in a battle over the facts. Each side attempts to outdo the other in acquiring the most respectable set of statistics on social consequences from the experts. Such disagreements do little to advance the main argument, which, as we have noted, is not a matter of fact, but a matter of value.

It would be possible to go on producing other consequential arguments used by the pro-Life[a] group. There is an argument from medical consequences, from psychological consequences, from ecological consequences, etc., etc. They all attempt to make the same point, which is that the consequences of a relaxation of our traditional stance on abortion are overwhelmingly bad. And in each case there is a proper kind of rebuttal which seeks to undermine the persuasive force of the particular argument at issue. Because of the limitations of space and time, perhaps we can assume we understand the thrust of the arguments of this group, and turn now to some of the arguments presented by the other side.

Some Pro-Life[c] Abortion Arguments

To an unbiased observer of the abortion debate, the arguments of the pro-Life[c] group will undoubtedly appear more varied and less monotonous. This is in some measure due to the fact that they are not limited to only one principled argument. Unlike the pro-Life[a] group, whose principle is the absolute or near absolute value of human life, the pro-Life[c] group has several such near absolute values—e.g., the inalienable right of women to control their bodies; the unquestionable right of consenting adults to engage in sexual activity without interference of any sort; and the absolute sovereignty of the individual human conscience.[6] Each of these gives rise to a principled argument in favor of the liberalization of abortion. Of course, there are also a battery of consequential arguments which are employed on this side of the debate, such as the argument from the life and health of the mother; from overpopulation; and the no unwanted or damaged child arguments.

Argument No. 4—An argument based on a woman's right to dominion over her body. Imagine the situation in which a geneticist has some high quality semen in his sperm bank, and he wishes to find a woman of suitable genetic qualities to complement it. Imagine further that you are the woman chosen by computer as the ideal genetic counterpart. Now suppose that instead of asking you to participate in his experiment, he simply kidnapped you and sedated you and then dispassionately and clinically introduced the sperm into your body thereby causing you to be pregnant. Finally assume that the geneticist intends to keep you a prisoner for the nine months of your pregnancy to insure that you will bring the newly conceived child to term. Surprising as it may seem, even under such unacceptable circumstances there are those who would say that should you escape you would have no right to abort the fetus (which was forced upon you) because of that fetus' inherent right to life. That would be to deny someone the right to dominion over her body simply because she is a woman and happens to be pregnant (against her will). Such a stand also reduces motherhood to a merely biological phenomenon by overlooking the importance of the voluntary in the gift of life.

But women are not subjected to violence only from strangers who would either experiment with them, or sexually assault them on the street (common rape). The litany of violences done to women within the so-called sanctity of marriage is legion. The drunken husband who impregnates his wife in a brutal way, the insensitive husband who selfishly takes no steps to control his passions or who threatens infidelity and thereby blackmails his wife into an unwanted pregnancy, are not uncommon cases. And always the sanctimonious anti-abortionists contend that the fact that the pregnancy was imposed on the woman by another and that the otherwise obvious right to dominion over the sexual uses of her body was grievously violated are not sufficient justification for an abortion. They hold that in all such cases the woman's right to the control of her body is in no way comparable to the fetus' right to life.

With respect to the latter point, it should be observed that the right to life does not mean that one's life can never be taken, but only that it cannot be taken unjustly. The question of abortion is then the question of whether the taking of prenatal life is ever justified. In those cases where the life in question has been coercively forced on the woman, it would seem that though she may nobly choose to accept responsibility for the life imposed on her, she is under no obligation to do so and therefore should not be forced to accept it. In all such cases abortion is not a violation of the right to life, because it is not an *unjust* taking of life.[7]

Rebuttal to Argument No. 4. The record shows that those who argue from the premise that a woman has a right over her body are not merely concerned with pregnancies which are forced on unwilling women. The argument is broadened to include the right of a once willing woman to change her mind and to unilaterally terminate her pregnancy (with or without the consent of her doctor) at any time prior to the birth of the child. For example, under the new law in California no recognition is given, prior to the birth of the child, to the rights of the father—even when he is the husband of the pregnant woman. On the basis of the principle of absolute dominion over their bodies, women have actually gone to court and have won the right to be the sole determiner of whether a child once conceived but yet unborn shall live. This marks a return to an unacceptable situation which existed in Imperial Rome, in which the paterfamilias alone determined whether the child would be brought to term or not. But in the 20th century, rather than place prenatal life under the arbitrary tyranny of a single male will, we see a move to insure that the tyranny will be that of the female. Today feminists ask for themselves the very thing which they and civilized society found intolerable in the past. This is hardly a rational request.

Then too, if the right to dominion over one's body is an absolute right, there seems to be nothing to prevent a mother from invoking it *after* the birth of the child. Should the only nourishment available for the child be its mother's milk, what is to prevent the mother from invoking her right to her own body to deprive the child of life-giving nourishment? Nothing in principle would prevent this from happening. Which means that the right to dominion over one's body is a principle which could be used to justify not only the abortion of the unborn but in certain instances (especially in underdeveloped countries) neglect of the already born. This shows that Argument No. 4 is based on a principle which knows no bounds, and which could logically and rationally be extended far beyond the abortion controversy. To accept the principle is, therefore, dangerous because of the possibility of one's being duped into accepting far more than the framers of Argument No. 4 deduce from it at this time. What of tomorrow?

Comment. In presenting Argument No. 4, I have tried to give it the most respectable form possible. It should be noted that in the heat of the public debate, many simply assume that a woman has the sole control of the life conceived within her up to the time of its delivery and birth. These same people claim that a woman may unilaterally terminate a pregnancy any time before that without concern for the interests or rights of any other person or social group. One could grant that a woman has a right over her body, but since she cannot of her own body become pregnant, once she does, it is evidence that a social act of wider dimensions than her individual will has already taken place. The proper time to unilaterally invoke the right to one's body is *be-*

fore a pregnancy occurs. After that the claim loses much of its rational appeal, except perhaps in those cases of violent coercion already mentioned. The conception of new life is not a totally private affair, but touches upon the rights and interests of many others. It is a social event, and as such cannot rationally be subject to a single will.[8]

Argument No. 5—An argument from the limits of legitimate interference. In his essay *On Liberty* (written in 1859), John Stuart Mill raised a question which continues to be of interest to contemporary man. At the very beginning of the fourth chapter, Mill asks: "What then is the rightful limit to the sovereignty of the individual over himself? Where does the authority of society begin?" Mill's answer has become part of the Western ideal governing the limits of governmental interference in the private affairs of its citizens, and has been traditionally used to differentiate the proper domain of the law from that of morality. He contends that, in a civilized society, the only reason for using force against a member of that society against his will is self-protection, i.e., to prevent the violation of the rights of another individual or harm from befalling the general good thus posing a threat to society itself. Interference with individual liberty is never justified simply to prevent someone from doing something we would prefer he didn't, or which we judge to be dangerous or harmful to him personally. In all such cases Mill counsels: ". . . there should be perfect freedom, legal and social, to do the act and stand the consequences."

In a pluralistic society like ours, in which Mill's "harm principle" is supposedly operative, one could justify interfering with the private decision to abort only if it could be shown that it violates the rights of some other citizens, or in some way threatens the general good of that society. Abortion does not violate the rights of a fellow citizen, because the fetus is not a bonafide member of society until it is born. While in the womb, the fetus is at best only a potential citizen. And who could possibly contend that an abortion performed in the private sector poses any kind of a threat to the public sector?

To allow for interference in such cases, not only violates the liberty of the individual it also blurs the line between the proper domain of the law and the order of morality. Even if one were to grant that abortion is immoral, this is not a sufficient justification for making it a concern of public policy or a matter of law. The law (and the governmental and social force behind it) can only promote moral good indirectly, for its primary aim is to prevent harm to others. In those cases where no harm to others is done, the State should practice a hands-off policy. While it may be true that many in our culture look on abortion as a terrible moral evil, and see each abortion performed as contrary to their private interests (moral or religious), it by no means follows that the use of legal force in behalf of those interests is justified. To give in to that kind of pressure would mark an important erosion of individual liberty, and place each individual in the republic at the mercy of interest groups more concerned with their partisan positions than with the promotion of individual freedom.

Rebuttal to Argument No. 5. It is by no means necessary to reject Mill's "harm principle" in order to reject the use to which it is put in Argument No. 5. Mill expressly states that societal and governmental interference in private matters is justified whenever the rights of others are violated. It simply will not do to say that in the case of abortion no rights are done harm because one is not a citizen until he is born. There are, after all, certain natural and inalienable rights which do not depend on one's being a citizen, and the right to life is one such. Even if one grants that citizenship comes at birth, it does not follow that one has no rights prior to being born. The American courts have consistently recognized the rights of the unborn,[9] so while it may be possible to interpret Mill theoretically in such a way as to deprive the unborn of the protection of the law, in practice (by legal precedent) the exact opposite has occurred. To accept Argument No. 5's use of Mill would, therefore, not only involve a questionable theoretical interpretation of the "harm principle," it would also undermine the traditional understanding and implementation of law in the United States.

In addition, Argument No. 5 seems to place law and morality into two watertight compartments. Now while it is certainly correct that not every matter of morality should be made a matter of law, it does not follow that matters of morality should never be subject to the sanctions of the law. We have laws against lying under oath, against murder, against theft and robbery etc., and each of these is as immoral as it is illegal, but for different reasons. An act is judged to be immoral because it involves a personal commitment on the part of the agent to be a certain kind of person, i.e., one who rejects the call to be fully human, and who acts in such a way as to make real trust and therefore real community impossible. On the other hand, any act which violates the rights of others should be judged illegal (although often it is not). Since one and the same act can very easily be subject to both sorts of evaluation, there is nothing wrong with an act being at once a moral matter as well as a legal one. Abortion is the kind of act which is clearly and properly the business of both morality and the law.

Comment. Because all parties to the abortion debate are operating with the assumption of a common commitment to pluralism, it becomes important to set down limits to forced uniformity. Failure to do so would be to make one's commitment to pluralism merely nominal but in no way real or practical. Put another way, one has to come to some acceptable way for handling dissent. If the only strategy is one of suppression, then pluralism is no longer prized and open debate itself becomes impossible. Small wonder then that the abortion debate should include an exchange on the proper limits of the private and public sectors. In fact, the exchange which follows could be looked at as a second attempt to tackle that same problem from another point of view.

Argument No. 6—An argument from the sovereignty of conscience. Undoubtedly there are many in our society who find abortion unacceptable on the basis of deeply held moral or religious convictions. For them it is a matter of conscience. As such, it is quite understandable that they work so tirelessly to practically implement their principles. Such zeal and commitment to principle are to be admired. However, conscience is sacred and inviolable not because of *what* it holds, but simply because it is conscience. It is not enough to be committed to one's personal conscience; one must also be committed to the right of another to follow his conscience even though it conflicts with one's own. Those who are against abortion are committed to their own consciences all right, but they have shown themselves to be particularly insensitive to the sovereignty of our consciences. How else are we to account for the repressive anti-abortion laws which completely dominated the scene until only recently? The time has come to re-establish a universal respect for conscience which does not hold a particular partisan conscience to be privileged. We do not ask the other side to give up their consciences in this matter for our sakes, but we do insist that they afford us the same courtesy. Indeed, we demand such respect as ours by right.

For example, some of us actually believe that the abortion decision is a strictly private matter between a woman and her physician, or between a couple and their doctor. As such it is governed solely by the consciences of the parties actually involved. To hold that the decision should be subject to the consciences of those not directly involved is to violate the rights of the participants and to make a mockery of our traditional commitment to the sanctity of individual conscience.

Finally, the first amendment of the Constitution prohibits the passing of any laws establishing religion. Any law which would impose a particular moral or religious belief regarding abortion on the citizenry would certainly be in violation of that amendment. But the traditional anti-abortion laws do just that and not only violate the sanctity of conscience, but also contravene the first amendment and are, therefore, clearly unconstitutional.

Rebuttal to Argument No. 6. The sovereignty of individual conscience is an important value in any democratic society, to be sure, but the practical meaning of that principle is certainly not beyond dispute. For example, it is important to determine whether and in what way "a man's right to follow his own conscience" differs from "a man's right to do anything he pleases." One gets the impression from Argument No. 6 that there is no difference at all. Could not the argument from conscience, as presented above, be used to forbid intervention in such things as the genocide of the Jews under Hitler, just because their extermination was a matter of conscience for the Nazis? This is not at all to say that the proponents of Argument No. 6 are just like the Nazis, but it is to say that their interpretation of the sovereignty of conscience affords us precious little defense against the kind of fanaticism exhibited in Hitler's Germany. A stand in favor of conscience which amounts to an endorsement of fanaticism will in the long run prove to be more beneficial to fanaticism than respectful of democratic freedom.

In the light of all that we have learned in dealing with the fanatics of the 20th century, it is simply untrue as Argument No. 6 proclaims that ". . . conscience is sacred and inviolable not because of *what* it holds, but simply because it is conscience." A person's conscience is obviously limited by the rights of others. I am at liberty to follow my conscience without interference only as long as the rights of others are not violated by my action. It may be true that I am obliged to follow my conscience even under those conditions, but in that situation I cannot claim that others have no right to interfere with me. The hallmark of the true man of conscience is his willingness to accept the consequences of those of his acts of conscience which affect others. In recent days, Martin Luther King, Jr. and the Berrigan brothers have exemplified the attitude of conscience proper to a pluralistic society, and each has paid a high personal price for his commitment.

Looked at from a more positive point of view, the commitment of civilized man to the sovereignty of conscience is not at all an open-ended endorsement of fanaticism. Rather it is based on the recognition that laws and social arrangements are not always just or ultimate. Whenever the laws and social mores violate the moral order, a man must be free to meet the higher demands of morality as revealed to him in conscience. The right to follow one's conscience is the inalienable right to be moral regardless of the demands of the law or society. It should never be interpreted as the right to be immoral.[10] All of which means that conscience is to be respected precisely because of its supposed morality, and not simply because it expresses an arbitrary desire of the individual.

Comment. Obviously Arguments No. 5 and 6 overlap. The former is based on a principle for determining the proper domain of the law, while the latter is based on a principle for determining the justifiable extent of individual conscience. Both end up attempting to draw a necessary line between the public and private domains. Because of the close affinity of the two arguments they are most often used in conjunction with one another in the abortion debate.

It is well to recall here that Arguments No. 4, 5, and 6 are *principled arguments*, and that each of them assumes the truth of the rebuttal given to Argument No. 1 above. Namely that it is arbitrary and contrary to the common opinion of mankind that a fetus is human in such a way as to be deserving from the start of the total respect due a human person. In short, the principle arguments of the pro-Life[c] group presuppose that the fetus is not human at each and every stage of its development. The acceptability of Arguments No. 4, 5 and 6 depends on whether one finds Argument No. 1 or its rebuttal more persuasive. Put another way, it would be unfair to accuse the proponents of Arguments No. 4, 5 and 6 of advocating the wanton taking of human life because, given their basic assumptions, that is not at all how they see the matter.

The litany of *consequential arguments* in favor of the pro-Life position is a long one. Instead of starting from a generally accepted principle from which a conclusion is deduced, all of these arguments begin with a certain unacceptable state of affairs in the real order and move to the conclusion that abortion is the obvious solution to the problem. I have selected only four from the list for consideration here, the argument from the unacceptable consequences to the life and health of the mother, the argument from overpopulation, and the argument from the unacceptable consequences to the child of being "unwanted," or "damaged."

Argument No. 7—An argument from the life and health of the mother. Located as it is at the center of life's mystery, the relationship between mother and child has been glorified in song and story from the beginning. It is all too easy to romanticize that relationship seeing it only as a beautiful model of selfless human love. But we must face the hard fact that we live in the real world, not an ideal one. In fact, situations arise, more often than we care to admit, in which the child in the womb is neither gift nor holy mystery but rather a severe threat to the life, health or general welfare of its mother. At such times romanticism and poetry are out of place, one must deal rationally with the hard facts of life. In the past, in all but the case of a life-against-life conflict between mother and child, the rights of the unborn have been pressed to the almost total exclusion of the rights of its mother. Only an unrealistic romanticism can account for the fact that in cases of conflict between fetal and maternal rights the rights of the unborn were automatically given priority. The time has most certainly come for us to take a more realistic stand.

When the life of the fetus produces a direct and immediate threat to the life of its mother, so that the two lives are in an irreconcilable mortal conflict to such a degree that medically it is impossible to save both; and when the mother is unwilling to sacrifice her life for the sake of the unborn, then direct abortive action against the unborn in keeping with accepted medical practice is the only humane and rational solution to the problem. If ever abortion was justified, it is in this case. Yet even in circumstances such as those described there is a minority which continues to argue in the abstract that the direct taking of a human life is never justified.

In the past the case of life-against-life is the only one in which maternal rights were seriously taken into account. But if abortion can be justified to protect the physical life of the mother, why can it not be justifiably used to protect those goods which we have traditionally taken to be equivalent to that life, such as physical health, the normal use of faculties, sanity and liberty? If bringing the child to term threatens the mother's physical well-being, her sanity, or her liberty, for all practical purposes we may consider these as threats to the life of the mother, and should logically be allowed to invoke the same solution as in the life-against-life conflict.

Unfortunately, the logic of this position has until recently not received the kind of support it deserves. If bringing a child to term would mean that its mother would be bedridden for the rest of her life, thus seriously infringing on her liberty, she is most certainly justified in having an abortion. If going through to the end with the pregnancy would seriously impair her faculties pushing her beyond her strength into insanity, who would deny that the child poses a significant threat to her life? Life for man is not merely a biological phenomenon, it requires that one be in full possession of his faculties. A threat to those qualities without which life is not worth the living must be practically taken as a threat to life itself, thus justifying the use of any means appropriate to the protection of life.

Finally, it should be said that no one is suggesting that a woman be forced to abort. She may always choose the loss of her life or one of its equivalents for the sake of her child. The point at issue is that she be allowed to choose. This means that there must at least be some other alternative open to her. Should she find that she cannot come up to the high standards of the romanticized view of motherhood which permeates our society, she should not feel or be made to feel that in aborting the child she has acted unjustifiably. She may not be as noble as some would like, but she has nothing about which to feel guilty.

Rebuttal to Argument No. 7. No doubt the life-against-life case is most agonizing, but we can be thankful that medical advances in our culture have made it a rare and always unnecessary predicament. Still because it remains a hypothetical possibility in our culture and a very real possibility in medically backward cultures, we must continue to attempt to articulate a morally acceptable way of handling it.

On the surface, the position of Argument No. 7 regarding the life-against-life conflict appears to be quite rational. But is it? It rails against the almost absolute value placed on the life of the fetus in the past, and then it baldly proceeds to place the same absolute value on the life of the mother. One is led to ask how what was condemned in one instance is justified in another. The fact of the matter is that there is no way in which one can choose between lives, when both are innocent. What seemed to the proponents of Argument No. 7 an unwarranted commitment to the life of the fetus was really a commitment to the equal value of human life wherever it occurs. All that is affirmed is that one may not take an innocent life to save another innocent life. The end does not justify the means. That this seemingly works more often to the detriment of the mother than of the fetus is just one more tragic aspect of an already agonizing situation. It is the proponents of Argument No. 7 who have made a choice of this life over that one, while steadfastly we refuse to redeem one at the expense of the other. It is they who have become sentimental and romanticized the situation, since they put forth no principle justifying the choosing between innocent lives. They remain totally arbitrary on this point.

Having accepted the fact that in the life-against-life case the end does not justify the means, the proponents of Argument No. 7 proceed to bring forth other cases which they suggest are really camouflaged equivalents of the life-against-life case. At least in a bonafide life-against-life case, the choice is between items of equal value, namely the innocent life of the mother versus the innocent life of the child. Indeed, it was this very real equivalence which made the choice so agonizing. But in the case of the health of the mother, her emotional stability, and her liberty, do we have a case of real equivalence? It is very hard to feign a life-against-life case, but once you allow these other values to weigh equally with the life of the fetus, you open the door to all sorts of simulation and pretending.

Finally, Argument No. 7 proves too much. For if one is able to take an innocent life justifiably for the reasons given, it is hard to see how these same reasons would not also justify infanticide when an already born child poses similar threats to its mother. The logic of Argument No. 7 is a slippery slope indeed. If you grant the life-against-life case, you are logically led to extend it to cases which are not life-against-life. And once you grant the right to move against the unborn, the same logic inexorably leads you to justify similar violence against the already born. Where will it end?

Comment. This exchange is typical of so many which have taken place between the two sides in the abortion debate. Operating from different principles it is almost, but not quite, as if the debate has turned into parallel monologues. The proponents of

Argument No. 7 have no difficulty in deciding the life-against-life case, precisely because their basic principle (Principle IV) is that fetal life is not equivalent to the more fully developed life of the mother. The decision is easy because the lives in conflict are not really considered to be equal. The opponents of Argument No. 7, on the other hand, see the conflict as between two innocent lives of absolutely equal value and, of course, in that case there is no justifiable way to decide between them.

Interestingly enough, each side makes an important point in this argument which is corroborated by common sense. The proponents of Argument No. 7 see no good reason to stand passively by while both lives are lost in the life-against-life case, when action would save at least one of them. This coincides perfectly with the honest moral convictions of the majority of mankind. On the other side, the opponents of Argument No. 7 also give expression to an equally basic human conviction, namely that there is something inherently wrong about pitting life against lesser goods on a basis of equality. Unfortunately as the arguments become more involved and sophisticated, both sides in the debate lose contact with the basic moral instincts of the human race, and inevitably end up each with its own set of more or less empty ratiocinations.[11]

Argument No. 8—An argument from overpopulation. In a world of limited and dwindling resources, unrestricted growth of population will most certainly outstrip the planet's capability of sustaining a life that is recognizably human. At first the human quality of life will be threatened, then it will be eroded, and eventually life itself will become extinct. The mechanisms of nature, when not interfered with by man, effectively control the size of the populations of subhuman life. The only real danger comes from man's propensity to procreate. Since it is unlikely that man will abstain from or appreciably lessen his sexual activity, the only viable alternative is to find a way to curtail the fecundity of human sexuality.

At present we have only four ways of doing that: (1) Surgical sterilization, by means of vasectomies, hysterectomies, the tying off of the Fallopian tubes and other such procedures. (2) Chemical contraceptives, e.g., pills, foams and ointments which prevent conception. (3) Mechanical contraceptives, such as diaphragms, condoms and other devices used to prevent the union of sperm and ovum. (4) Abortion, which is the destruction of life already conceived, by means of chemicals, mechanical suction, or other appropriate surgical procedures.

The alternatives are obvious: We either employ the means at our disposal to limit the growth of the human population, or we face the certainty of extinction. Under less drastic circumstances it might make sense to debate the merits of each of the methods of population control. That is a luxury we simply cannot afford now that time is running out and the survival of the human race is in the balance. We are faced here with a life-against-life case of a new sort, the lives of those already born are pitted against the lives of the yet to be born. It is obvious that in such a conflict the lives of the already born are rightfully granted priority.

In such dire circumstances, it simply will not do to employ means which are not effective, for that amounts to doing nothing. But of the four means at our disposal, only abortion has shown itself to be an effective method of "birth control."[12] Surgical sterilization, while growing in its acceptability in the advanced countries of the world, is not generally accepted and involves a long list of psychological hang-ups. Chemical and mechanical contraceptives infringe on the natural quality of sexual relations and are therefore shunned or used only in half-hearted and hence ineffective ways. This leaves only abortion as an effective means of population control.

Those who object to this conclusion had better think twice about the matter. For if we do not freely and voluntarily stem the growth of population on our planet, those charged with the social order will have no choice but to employ coercion in achieving acceptable population levels. In the crunch, our only option will be to implement population control voluntarily or to have it forced upon us. The former solution may not be an unalloyed good, but it is certainly far and away the lesser of two evils.

Rebuttal to Argument No. 8. The proponents of Argument No. 8 talk as if the population problem were a simple problem and as if abortion were the only solution. It would be much more accurate to say that each nation and culture is faced with a specific sort of population problem, and that the world is faced with a related series of population *problems*. Some demographers stress the immediate problem of births in underdeveloped countries. Some speak of the pollution problem which results not only from the number of people but also from their patterns of consumption and disposal of waste. Some counsel short term tactics, others, policies for the long run. In such a complicated situation, it is simple-minded to propose abortion as *the* solution. What we need is much more research into population growth and the whole constellation of its allied problems.

Since we are talking primarily about the United States, it is interesting to note that the U.S. Census Bureau announced that zero population growth was reached in the United States in December of 1972. Now while it is true that the overall number of people in the United States will continue to increase because the children of the post-War baby boom have entered childbearing years, it remains true that the loudly proclaimed people explosion has not materialized. This should be sufficient reason to make us all wary of population "predictions." At least we should not allow ourselves to be stampeded into an abortion policy which might prove to have been unnecessary.

The problem may not be a matter of numbers so much as of population density. Certainly insofar as that is true, abortion is not even a bad solution, it is no solution at all. In Holland the population density is 1000 persons per square mile, in the United States it is 54. For a variety of economic, social, political and personal reasons the majority of our people want to live in the already over-crowded cities. We have 70% of our population living on 1% of the land. Our problem is not one of numbers but of an intelligent distribution of those numbers. It is hard to see how abortion can be shown to be an effective solution to the problem of distribution.

But even if one were to grant that the number remains the main problem, it by no means follows that abortion (voluntary or forced) is the only solution. One important factor in our reaching zero population growth has been the new awareness among our people of childbearing age of the problem. We should inaugurate an information program which makes wider use of mass media to encourage late marriages, responsible parenthood, and to enhance the prestige of the single state among our people. Such an effort would have a profound effect on our attitudes. And in the area of sexual behavior, attitude is perhaps the most important factor. In any event, it is irrational to hold out abortion as the only solution to our problem.

Finally, the proponents of Argument No. 8 make much of the threat of extinction and hold out survival as the topmost value. The history of man is replete with episodes in which men chose to die rather than to accept the kind of life which was offered to them. We are a people sprung from forebears who proclaimed: "Give me liberty or give me death!" We do them no honor if, in the 20th century, we settle for mere survival. The question is not at all whether we will survive, but whether we shall have the courage and fortitude to survive as a people committed to liberty and justice, that is as a people who steadfastly refuse to accept life for themselves at the expense of the innocent and helpless among them. Those who would attempt to motivate us through fear should beware of such tactics, for fear is a harsh taskmaster who makes no distinctions. Fear of extinction is not easily controlled once motivated, and it could all too easily be used to justify violence not only against the unborn, but against one's fellows. In such circumstances might makes right, and human community is impossible.

Comment. Perhaps nowhere more than in the population argument do the participants in the abortion debate have recourse to expert testimony and the use of statistics. Since both sides have their own experts, it is difficult to know just what the facts are. I have tried to avoid getting too deeply involved in the morass of contradictory population statistics for fear of never getting myself extricated.[13]

Argument No. 9—The unwanted child argument. Parenthood is undoubtedly the most demanding enterprise open to human beings. It is a truism that only parents who have raised a child are aware of the extent of that commitment. In a sense, it is unfortunate that so exacting and relentless a task can be embarked upon so easily. But however unfortunate it may be for the parents, it can prove to be even more devastating for the child. Thanks to the findings of psychology and the social sciences, we are now more alert to the fact that when the burdens of parenthood become so crushing that the father and mother repent their parenthood, the destructive effects on the impressionable child are disastrous. All too many children bear physical and psychological scars on this account, and some have deformed and twisted personalities until their dying day. When we come to speak of a child's right to life, we should now also include the right of each child to be really wanted by his parents. No child should be forced to live his life in circumstances in which he feels constant repudiation from his parents.

There is little that can be done when prospective parents originally want a child and only come to reject it later. But in those situations in which prospective parents have unwittingly stumbled into an unwanted pregnancy and have neither the willingness nor the capability of assuming the demanding role of loving parenthood, an abortion is in order. Life is a gift, and there is something truly inappropriate about conferring it against one's will. Certainly there will always be those who rejoice in the conception of new life and who await its birth in joyful hope. And that is as it should be. Indeed, it should be no other way. But when the new life has been inadvertently conferred, when it occasions only remorse and despair, it is cruel and inhuman to condemn the child to life. Human life is more than its biology, it requires certain basic social and familial conditions as well. When these are absent, the life in question is no longer a beneficent gift but has become a cruel punishment. In such cases, unfortunate as it may be, abortion becomes less cruel than life.

Rebuttal to Argument No. 9. If the argument from overpopulation plays on our fears, Argument No. 9 plays on our sympathy. But what sense does it make to add to the misery of the unwanted child by physically assaulting him while in the womb? That simply compounds his misfortunes and makes him even more deserving of sympathy. But leaving sympathy aside, Argument No. 9 conveniently ignores two very important aspects of human life. First, experience teaches us that it is no easy thing to know what you want, what you *really* want. And second, human existence is a temporal existence and no accurate account can be given of it if that temporality is ignored.

How often have you had to say to yourself: "I don't know why I did that, I really didn't want to"? We all have urges, drives and moods which seem to lead us to what we want. But once there, we find that it was not really what we wanted at all. Sometimes our regret is immediate, but at other times it may be delayed a week, a month, a year or more. The point to be made is that there is no automatic guarantee that what we want now is going to hold up and be in the end what we really wanted. Argument No. 9 ignores this obvious aspect of human life and assumes that there is no problem at all in deciding that a child is unwanted. It refuses to face up to the ambiguity which permeates our lives.

That ambiguity is partially due to the fact that we do not live our total lives in the present moment. We are beings who come to the fullness of our humanity developmentally, in time. This means that no single moment can be taken as decisive in isolation from the rest of our lives. Now it is common medical knowledge that with the onset of pregnancy there is a profound hormonal change in the woman which quite often causes acute depression. Being faced simultaneously with the rigors of parenthood, the discomforts of pregnancy, the psychological shock of loss of figure, and the uncertainties of the effect the pregnancy will have on her sexual relations can all but overwhelm a woman already feeling depressed. It would be in no way surprising if at that time she said she didn't want the child, although she might very well mean that she isn't looking forward to all those other consequences of her pregnancy. It is also common knowledge that later in a normal pregnancy the woman takes on the glow of radiant physical health, which is generally accompanied by a complete reversal of mood. Now she looks forward to the birth of her child and begins to feel the joys traditionally associated with motherhood. Now, since each of these is a stage in a normal pregnancy, how does one determine which one expresses what the mother really wants? Put another way, if one were to abort the child while its mother was in the first state, could he be sure that he did what she really wanted and that subsequently she will not repent of his having taken it?

Of all the arguments in favor of abortion, this one is the most dangerous. For once the category of being "unwanted" is taken as decisive, no one of us is safe. If our supposed right to be wanted is a condition for our existence, we had better all become hermits. For if one lives among his fellows, there will inevitably be moments when he is unwanted by them. Who among us has not experienced moments when he no longer wanted to care for an aged parent, or sacrifice for an ailing spouse? But we know that such moments of unwanting pass, and that even as we are complaining about our burdens in our heart of hearts we really want to continue to shoulder them. And we really want to because we are well aware of the fact that the day must surely come when we shall be similarly unwanted, and then we shall have to depend on the courage of others to keep their unwanting moments from being decisive.

Comment. It should be noted that the unwanted child argument can be taken in two ways. If one stresses the fact that each child has a right to be wanted, the argument is *principled.* If, on the other hand, being unwanted is viewed as an unacceptable situation which only abortion can ameliorate, then the argument is *consequential.* The final argument we shall consider is one such and it is concerned with a specific kind of unwanted child, i.e., one that is retarded or damaged.

Argument No. 10—The damaged child argument. Once upon a time, every couple which conceived new life was forced to live through the nine months of pregnancy in agonizing uncertainty about the health of the unborn. Would it be born healthy and whole, or would it be numbered among the predictable percentage of monstrosities, mongoloids, severely retarded and otherwise damaged children? There was no way of knowing; all that could be done was to wait and see.

Fortunately, the phenomenal advances of medical science and the establishment of a new branch of medicine devoted exclusively to the care of prenatal life (fetology) have changed all that. It is now possible for prospective parents to determine well in advance of birth whether the life they have generated is damaged, and oftentimes also the extent of the damage. When the diagnostic tests are positive and indicate damage to the fetus, the parents are in a position to decide whether they will bring the baby to term or not. In all such cases, the freedom of the parents to decide should be safeguarded, but it is simply irrational to force such parents to bring a damaged child into the world against their will. (See Argument No. 9 regarding an unwanted child.)

For those who are appalled by this prospect of aborting defective fetuses, it might be well to recall that fully one-fourth of all the fertilized ova are naturally aborted because of some defect. This should cause those who continue to claim that fetal life is human from the start some real concern. One out of four conceptions never come to term without external interference of any sort. Our improved knowledge simply allows us to extend nature's capability of dealing with defective fetuses. Men interfere with nature to improve plant yield, to breed better livestock, and to secure more favorable weather. Why can we not interfere to improve on nature's rejection of defective humans?

Interestingly enough, those who abhor the abortion of the defective seem to have little or no compunction about suggesting that society and the law have the right to place intolerable burdens of self-sacrifice on their parents. When you deprive the parents of a defective child in the womb of the right to dispose of it, you are in effect insisting that *they* assume all the burdens and sacrifices which usually befall the families of such children once born. You sentence them to untold agonies, not the least of which might be financial ruin. These are interpersonal familial burdens and the state acts beyond its competence when it attempts to legislate in this area. After all, the prospective parents themselves know better than anyone else the limits of their strength, it should be for them to make the decision. There is something terribly wrong with vesting the decision in the hands of those who will play no part in bearing the terrible burden of a defective child on a day by day basis.

Nor will it do to suggest that the state has a right to act in this area if it puts state facilities for the damaged and retarded at the disposal of the parents. This in no way relieves the parents of burdens. Leaving aside the consideration of expense to the taxpayers, it is a great personal sacrifice to have to give up your child to an institution, or to have to continually take him to such facilities on an out-patient basis. Undoubtedly there are those who feel themselves capable of assuming such lifelong burdens. For their sake the state should be obliged to provide proper facilities. But there is no reason to suppose that the existence of such facilities imposes an obligation on those parents who choose not to need them, because they have aborted a defective fetus.

Finally, a word should be said about the defective child himself. While the examples of Helen Keller and others are a source of wonder for us all, there are millions of others who live lives which are completely unheralded because they are so completely subhuman. We generally keep them out of sight, but they do exist and they exist without the slightest trace of humanness. While we do not suggest that all such already born should be summarily dispatched, it does seem rational to suggest that we use our improved medical knowledge to avoid adding to their number.

Rebuttal to Argument No. 10. For the record, it should be noted that the medical advances so highly praised in the argument were originally aimed at improving the quality of prenatal life. The use to which such skills are being put to serve the personal interests of the parents cannot be helped, perhaps, but one gets an uneasy feeling when lifesaving and life-improving techniques are perverted to serve the destruction of life, for whatever reason. If that is the use to which it is going to be put, just how many more advances in lifesaving knowledge can we stand?

But what is more disturbing about Argument No. 10 is the way in which it condones abortion whenever the unborn is defective. The question of how defective is never brought up. The only criterion used was that the defect present the parents with burdens they are unwilling to accept. In that case, how could we logically prevent the argument from being used to justify abortion both in cases of slight defects (which are unacceptable to the parents) as well as in the cases of birth defects which would prevent the child from evidencing any signs of humanness? The argument seems to rest more on the attitude of the parents than on the severity of the defect.

What is more, it is the attitude of prospective parents of defective children whose fears are in some degree of the unknown.

The late Pearl Buck, whose child was retarded from phenylketonuria, speaks from actual experience when she says: "My child's life has not been meaningless. She has indeed brought comfort to many people. True she has done it through me, yet without her I would not have had the means of learning how to accept the inevitable sorrow, and how to make that acceptance useful to others. Would I be so heartless as to say that it has been worthwhile for my child to be born retarded? Certainly not, but I am saying that even though gravely retarded it has been worthwhile for her to have lived. A retarded child, a handicapped person, brings its own gift to life, even to the life of normal human beings. That gift is comprehended in the lessons of patience, understanding, and mercy, lessons which we all need to receive and to practice with one another, whatever we are. For this gift bestowed upon me by a helpless child, I give my thanks."[14] And speaking to the Ohio legislature in 1971, Mrs. Rosalie Craig, herself a parent of a retarded child said: "There has not been a single organization of parents of mentally retarded children that has ever endorsed abortion."[15] Perhaps they all know something we don't.

Like so many of the arguments put forth in support of abortion, this one also lacks any logical control to keep it from going far beyond its original limits. If the attitude of others is what determines one's right to life, in the light of Argument No. 10 how could we protect those damaged after birth when their disability presents those around them with burdens they are unwilling to bear? The argument seems to put the lives of the senile, the victims of automobile and industrial accidents, and disabled veterans all in jeopardy. Since we are all more or less defective—no one after all is perfect—if we endorse this argument we are sealing our own doom. Life will no longer be an inalienable right at all, but will depend on the willingness of others to sacrifice themselves for it. In the absence of such willingness, not only the right to life but life itself will be forfeit. We have not done enough to help instill a willingness to sacrifice for each other, or else this argument would never be taken seriously. But things are never so bad that they cannot get worse. And worse they will certainly get if Argument No. 10 prevails. For in that case we will not only not be engendering self-sacrifice, we shall be publicly disclaiming it as a value in our lives together. In that event we shall be promoting 1984, or worse.

Comment. It is hard to know for sure whether this exchange belongs among the abortion arguments, or whether it would more properly fit in the next chapter as prenatal euthanasia. I have chosen to include it here because of its affinity to the unwanted child argument.

A Postscript

It was never my intention to catalogue *all* of the arguments used in the abortion debate. I chose those which seemed to me to be most telling and most interesting. I am reasonably sure that both sides will find my presentation of their arguments defective. All I can say is that since I did not want to become a partisan in the debate myself, I tried to present each argument and each rebuttal as objectively and forcefully as I could. The reader must decide the merits of the case for himself. What I was at some pains to establish, however, was that no argument in the abortion debate goes unchallenged or is without its own appropriate response. That is, after all, in the very nature of a debate. But despite all the effort at point and counterpoint the matter remains in large measure rationally inconclusive and a certain sense of ambiguity prevails. There are intelligent men on both sides of the controversy, which means that rationality and intelligence are not sufficient to settle the matter.[16] This is, as we shall see, not without deep significance for us.

Chapter Three

ELEMENTS OF THE EUTHANASIA DEBATE

THE word "euthanasia" belongs with other such words as "eulogy" and "euphonic." A eulogy is a speech in which you praise someone by saying pleasant things about him; melodious and pleasant sounds are characterized as being euphonic. Taken literally, euthanasia is a good, pleasant or fortunate death. The word originally had no note of violence or evil about it. To many it has become a horrible word, a synonym for the unjustified taking of a human life which its advocates euphemistically call "mercy death," but which in reality is the equivalent of murder. If we were to use it in that sense in the debate, we would find it difficult to find any proponents for euthanasia since no one would be willing to publicly debate in favor of murder. In fact, one reason there is a current revival of the debate on the matter is because there are growing numbers of people who have returned to the original sense of "euthanasia" and see it not only as a good, but even as a right. A man has a right to as good, pleasant and fortunate a death as we can manage for him. Since it is hard to imagine how there could be any disagreement on that point, the debate is more precisely over the limits to be placed on the ways and means of achieving that end.

Since everyone is agreed on the value of a felicitous death, the euthanasia controversy is not really marked by the same sort of acrimony as the abortion debate. There is a sense in which helping someone to die well is attractive to everyone, while abortion is never presented as *attractive*, not even by those who deem it to be allowable and necessary. The fact that euthanasia can be presented as attractive to the basic sensibilities of the ordinary man in ways in which abortion cannot is, to my mind, the most significant difference between the two acts. This precludes putting them in the same class and severely undermines the much quoted "slippery slope," "camel's nose" or "wedge" argument that abortion inevitably leads to euthanasia.[1]

A second difference between the two debates is that unlike the abortion debate in which the traditional Catholic position is the most conservative one and hence the target for all the others, in this one the Catholic tradition is among the more liberal positions. I admit that there are many Catholic authors who remain rigid on the question of euthanasia. In fact the shortest treatment of euthanasia that I ran across was from one such author. It said simply: "Little need be said on this topic. If administered by oneself, euthanasia is suicide. If administered by another without the victims consent, it is murder. If administered by another with the victim's consent or cooperation, it is suicide and murder."[2] But such logically perfect and humanly arid presentations can never do justice to a tradition which has always held that a man need not employ extraordinary means to save himself, not even from a curable disease to say nothing of an incurable one.[3] Obviously this means that a little more needs to be said than was said in the shortest treatment. This time rather than present a string of arguments pro and con, as we did with abortion, let us consider some of the important elements around which euthanasia arguments cluster.

The Right to Live vs. The Right to Choose to Die

Christians, and other religious people, have at their disposal in this debate, as in the other one, an argument which is so conclusive that it can be called "the" argument. But they can't use it, except when talking to one another, because it violates the common commitment to pluralism in the public forum which is one of the basic assumptions of the debate. According to that traditional argument, God is the Lord of life and death, and he alone has dominion over it. This automatically precludes any justification for taking the human life of oneself or of another. If this is taken for granted, one can see why so many Catholic authors have so little to say about euthanasia. In the light of "the" argument, what more could possibly be said?

Nothing, by those who accept it. But there are many in our country who deny the existence of God; for them the argument is simply inconclusive. And even among the God-fearing, one finds a growing reluctance to treat the matter all that simply. While it may be true that a man cannot presume to hold dominion over the lives of others (thus ruling out the taking of the life of another) who but he has dominion over his own life? The traditional response suggests that a man's life is not really his own, but is rather something he has on loan from God and over which he holds but a temporary stewardship. The conditions of that stewardship allow him to put his life to any use he chooses, but always in the knowledge that he will eventually be asked to give an account of his stewardship. Still, he may not destroy that life, because it is not really his by right.

But how can that be? Is it not equally traditional to view life as a precious gift from God? If so, it is in the nature of a gift that it really be given with no strings attached. The recipient of a gift receives along with the gift complete dominion over it. If he does not, it was not a gift that he received, but something loaned or leased to him for his use. Since Christians feel that it has been revealed that life is truly a *gift* from God (Cf. Gen. 2:7; Ps. 104:30; James 1:17), it is possible for some of them to hold that because it is truly a gift, suicide and the act of freely choosing death for oneself need not be interpreted as violating any sort of divine dominion. Suicide may still be unacceptable for other reasons, it is just that the divine dominion argument no longer seems capable of establishing that fact beyond all doubt. If so, the debate is on!

A man may attempt to end his life by his own hand for a great variety of reasons. Some commit suicide to avoid facing public disgrace, financial ruin, or apprehension and conviction by the law enforcement authorities. Such suicides do not really enter into the euthanasia debate because they are attempts to avoid the consequences of one's own acts. A second group of suicides stems from insanity, deep emotional difficulties, and the release of pent up feelings of aggression or guilt in an act of self-destruction. They are usually seen as results of social and psychic inadequacy and in most cases are judged to be acts for which the individual is not fully responsible. As such they do not enter directly into the euthanasia controversy.

Suicide and euthanasia do come together in those cases in which a man takes his own life in order to secure a more felicitous, peaceful, dignified and painless death than seemed to be in store for him otherwise. In such circumstances does a man have the right to take his own life? Does he have the right to seek the cooperation of others in such activity, and if he does, do they have the right to cooperate?[4]

Having had the divine dominion argument ruled out of the public debate, those who would answer negatively bring forth two other arguments which have been traditional. The first suggests that it is against the laws of man's nature for him to self-destruct. Such an action goes contrary to the law of self-preservation. Secondly, since man is a social being, it is also improper to suggest that he may unilaterally end his life without consideration for the good of the community of which he is a part, or of the rights and interests of individuals who depend on him.

To which the other side responds that the law of self-preservation which acts instinctively in animals is a function of consciousness in man. A man is not blindly driven to self-preservation at all costs. He may judge that a felicitous death is the most significant way to preserve the integrity of the human element in his existence. If so, then his act of self-destruction is but a more highly sophisticated expression of the law of self-preservation. As for the rights of the community, family and dependents, they are neither absolute nor unlimited. It is hard to see what good the community could claim as justification for imposing a more unpleasant death than is necessary on one of its members against his will. The claims of family and friends certainly do not extend beyond what can rationally be expected. They have no right to expect one to endure a torturous death when other alternatives are available.

Direct Killing vs. Allowing To Die

Having noted that there is a disagreement over whether a man in principle has a right to end his own life, it should not surprise us to find that there is a subsequent disagreement on the ways and means to be used in securing a dignified human death. Many who think it is always objectionable to overtly act against innocent human life find nothing wrong with a passive inactivity which allows the terminally ill patient to die more peacefully. This is in accord with the moral sentiments of the ordinary man, who judges that there is an important difference between actually doing something and doing nothing to prevent something from happening. Few doctors feel themselves to be ordinary men, but many of them feel that their Hippocratic oath prevents such inactivity with respect to terminally ill patients.

Prolonging Living vs. Prolonging Dying. The miracles of modern medicine have contributed to an attitude on the part of both doctors and patients which, if not carefully watched, degenerates into human arrogance. Patients entertain such unrealistic expectations about doctors that they refuse to face up either to the possibility or to the inevitability of death. It is very easy, under such circumstances, for the doctors to attempt to live up to the unreal expectations of their patients. More medical advances just make patients more unrealistic which in turn invites their doctors to be even more zealous in fulfilling those expectations. And so round and round we go. In such an atmosphere the medical profession becomes prostituted to crisis situations (emergency life-saving) and preventive medicine is all but neglected. We pay doctors to cure our diseases rather than to prevent them. In such circumstances, it is not unexpected that all talk of euthanasia is rejected by the medical profession.

Like it or not, we have to admit that this frenzy for lifesaving medicine on the part of patients and doctors has now reached the stage where medical technology is not only being used to prolong life but also to prolong the act of dying. That in itself is not objectionable since some may want to have their dying extended. But it is ludicrous to deny that there is an observable point at which lifesaving becomes death-prolonging. With the famous Protestant theologian Karl Barth, we might well ask ". . . whether this kind of artificial prolongation of life does not amount to human arrogance, whether the fulfillment of medical duty does not threaten to become fanaticism, reason folly, and the required assisting of human life a forbidden torturing of it?"[5]

Ordinary vs. Extraordinary Lifesaving. One of the arguments most often used against the contemporary fanaticism of lifesaving medicine (along with its experimentation on humans with and without their consent[6]) is not at all new, but has been with us for some time. It is the traditional distinction made by Catholic moralists between ordinary and extraordinary lifesaving techniques. A man may be obliged to use ordinary means to sustain his life, but he need not avail himself of any means which is extraordinary. And in this context extraordinary signifies any medicine, treatment or operation which cannot be obtained or used without excessive expense, pain or inconvenience to the patient or others, or which if used would not offer a reasonable hope of benefit to the patient.[7]

Obviously the ordinary/extraordinary means argument can be used to good purpose in the euthanasia debate, but it is effective only in situations in which the patient voluntarily asks to be allowed to forego further medical help. It has no effect on the movement of thought once the argument turns to the acceptability of direct acts against the life of a terminally ill patient. To say that a man has the right to forego help is not the same thing as saying that he has a right to take an overdose of sleeping pills, or that he may be quietly gassed. In order to make that kind of move in the argument, one has to go beyond even the most liberal of the traditional Catholic positions.

Naturally those who want to do this are not without their own arguments. If one grants that a man can refuse or reject medical assistance in order to insure a felicitous death, he has in principle granted the case for euthanasia. To nit-pick over the means seems shallow and unfeeling when everyone concerned with the case yearns for a quick and humane end. The patient wants it. His family wants it. Let us suppose that even his doctor wants it but is constrained by the threat of legal prosecution. In such circumstances it is the sheerest nonsense to serve some empty principle and to ignore the real needs and desires of persons. We would be more compassionate to a wounded animal. Yet in the case of our fellow human beings we have allowed an empty distinction (between direct and indirect euthanasia) to carry the day.

One important factor in this matter has been the natural revulsion experienced in this century due to the compulsory euthanasia practiced in Nazi Germany during World War II. But that is beside the point. No one is advocating compulsory euthanasia; the question being asked is whether a man has a right to take direct action against his own life or to delegate another to do so in order to secure a peaceful and humane death. Compulsory euthanasia or genocide have nothing whatsoever to do with it. The time has come for the people of the United States to insist that their right to die with human dignity be respected. We must become as concerned about the quality of death as we are becoming about the quality of life.

As the situation now stands anyone tired of his life can end it at will because, if he is serious, there is just no way to stop him. One is forced to deal with cases of successful suicide after the fact. Such cases usually elicit strong social disapproval, but the truth of the matter is that suicide is not generally a crime in the

United States. Put another way, since there is no law against it, a man seems to have a right to commit suicide if he wants to and is ingenious enough to pull it off. Of course, if he fails he may find himself forced by law to undergo psychiatric treatment. What is so curious about this situation is that it seems to confer on a special group (*successful* suicides) the right to take direct action against their lives without penalty. True, those who aid or abet someone in committing suicide are not free from criminal prosecution, but that only means that to help a suicide is criminal but to commit suicide is not. The question which this immediately raises is this: How can it possibly be a crime to aid and abet a man in the performance of an act which is not itself a crime?

The irrationality of the situation does not end there, it can be pushed one step further. By what right or logic do we confer on healthy persons the right to directly take their own lives if they care to, and refuse that same right to the terminally ill? We can always grant that there is some logic and consistency in saying that one cannot aid a potential suicide either when he is healthy or when he is terminally ill. But since this bit of logical consistency comes a little late in the game, it cannot possibly redeem the irrationality of our having laws against direct euthanasia. Such laws unjustly discriminate against the terminally ill when their sickness is physical but not when it is psychic or emotional. These inconsistencies are easily avoided by admitting the merits of the case for direct and voluntary euthanasia.

Some Haunting Difficulties

If the case is all that clear, how are we to account for the fact that killing terminally sick people continues to not be very popular? Perhaps it is that when all is said and done there remain some ambiguities about the whole enterprise. Let's consider some of them now.

For Whose Sake? It is a noble thing to take a stand on principle. It is a noble thing to press for the rights of others. But when those who stand on principle and promote the rights of some group are themselves served by what they promote it is wise to take a closer look. The arguments put forth for direct euthanasia turn our attention toward the terminally ill who would benefit. But they are not the *only* beneficiaries. Those relatives who live on could conceivably have a vested interest in an early demise for their loved one. Death would free them from the burdens of care and concern which they might otherwise owe the deceased. If the way in which we treat old people in this country *before* they are terminally ill is any indication of what is in our hearts, then there can be no question of what will be in our hearts once they are ill. Our overriding disposition is to rid ourselves of what is burdensome.[8] In such circumstances are we to be trusted? Is there not an irreconcilable conflict of interests here?

This creates other difficulties, for which of the beneficiaries is to have the final say in this matter of when and how the life in question is to be terminated? This is relatively unimportant, perhaps, so long as there is agreement among the sick and healthy involved in the decision. But should a disagreement arise, what then? In such a contest of wills, the healthy person has the obvious advantage, and this brings the voluntariness of euthanasia into serious question.

How Voluntary is Voluntary? We have all witnessed actions which were presented as voluntary about which we had serious doubts. George McGovern in the campaign of 1972 voluntarily dumped Senator Eagleton. The decision was his and his alone, and he assured everyone that he made it voluntarily. Americans have seen their POW's make statements which purported to be voluntary acts, and again we are assured that no violence was used to get the statements from them. If this sort of thing is what the proponents of direct euthanasia mean by "voluntary euthanasia," it would be very hard, indeed, to distinguish what they propose from that whole class of actions which are coerced, not physically but by means of psychological and social pressure. In fact, the question to be put to those who favor direct euthanasia is this: How can you guarantee the true voluntariness of euthanasia given the special circumstances in which it occurs?

By the time a euthanasia decision is at hand, the patient has usually been subjected to intense physical pain or stress. Psychologically he has had to face the possibility of his death as well as the possibility of his lingering and becoming a burden on his family. At such a time he is particularly vulnerable to feelings of guilt or shame for having become a burden on others. How voluntary is the euthanasia decision in such circumstances? Certainly the patient is no match for an artful practitioner in the arts of persuasion who is himself healthy and in command of his faculties. The potentials for manipulation in such a situation are boundless.

What if the Diagnosis is Mistaken? The discussion thus far has taken the terminal stage of the illness for granted. The judgment that someone is incurably ill and the description of what his remaining days on earth will be like are basically medical judgments based on the experience of the doctor. That means that their validity is a function of the skill and experience of the physician. Since physicians generally cover a wide spectrum of medical competence, there is always the chance that the medical judgment is erroneous. Euthanasia is an irrevocable response to a medical judgment, which means that there is no recourse if a mistake has been made. In the light of this possibility, one should be very cautious indeed.

What about the Doctor-Patient Relationship? If euthanasia were to become an accepted medical practice, it would certainly have a profound effect on the relation between patient and doctor. The patient would always be wondering whether the doctor was *really* doing all he could to save his life, since it would be so easy to solve the problem by means of euthanasia. The lifesaving effort would always be taking place in the shadow of that other alternative, if things didn't work out. In such circumstances the patient would lose confidence in his physician, and as we now know that could have serious effects on his health and the prognosis for recovery.

Should euthanasia become a national policy, it seems likely that the sense of urgency which now characterizes medical research could not be sustained. The all-out efforts which we have witnessed against cancer, leukemia, muscular dystrophy would be appreciably lessened. Funds might not be so readily available, and this could result in a slowing down of those medical advances which have so enhanced our lives.

Obviously, we all want to help those dying in our midst as much as possible to have a pain-free and peaceful death. But we should not allow our natural sentiments in this matter to be used to stampede us into a euthanasia policy which would not insure the freedom of the patient; which would subject the patient to severe pressures precisely at a time when he is least able to cope with them; and which would generally undermine the good medical practice and high medical standards which we now enjoy in this country.

The Debate Goes On

There is really no need to go on with this, because the euthanasia debate, like the abortion debate, is endless. Admittedly, our brief examinations of each debate in no way do them justice. The debates themselves are as much a product of the creativity of modern man as are his skyscrapers and spaceships. Those engaged in them are as energetic, skillful, and devoted as our technologists. In fact they are, in a real sense, the technologists of the modern right to life debate. One cannot help admiring them for their technology, but as I have already suggested, there is something wrong-headed and unacceptable about allowing them to have the last word. We have a penchant for thinking that we must leave it to experts to solve our problems. I personally remain unconvinced that the doctors, lawyers, demographers, sociologists, psychologists, philosophers, priests, theologians, and professional liberals are the right experts with regard to abortion and euthanasia. But I am absolutely convinced that to attempt to solve these problems in public debate within a pluralistic society is futile because of the tragic flaw we have introduced into the Western ideal of democracy. The time has come to leave the debates behind and to explore the significance of my convictions.

Chapter Four

AN ALTERNATIVE TO DEBATING THE
RIGHT TO LIFE

I T is generally assumed that when confronted with the right to life debate one is obliged to take one side or the other. I hope that what has preceded has conveyed something of the ambiguity which such a stand entails, and that the reader is now open enough to at least entertain, if not accept, another alternative. To my mind, there are two things which invite such a move. First, I know of no one (absolutely no one) who has been faced with a life-death decision who made that decision solely or even principally on the basis of the arguments presented in the debate. And secondly, due to their fervor in producing such arguments, the partisans in the debate are generally unaware of the other than rational factors which form and fashion their positions. They do not accept their arguments as conclusive because they are rational; rather they claim they are rational because they already accept them as conclusive.

Catholics are the ones usually singled out by their opponents as having nonrational (religious) elements hidden behind their arguments. For some strange reason, the Catholics vehemently deny this charge, as if to match the quality of their opponents' arguments which is supposedly purely rational. If that were the case, then we should expect their arguments to be conclusive. But they are not conclusive either, because *all* the arguments in the debate rest on other than rational grounds; it is just that everyone seems afraid to admit it. To do so would be to seriously undercut the respectability of the debate in a culture like ours which worships at the shrine of rationality.

A Pox on Both Their Houses

It is my contention that the respectability of the right to life debate can be questioned not only because it dishonestly hides its nonrational roots, but also because in some very serious respects it fails as rationality. This is obvious if one considers some of the clearly false assumptions which *both* sides to the debate make.

The first false assumption is that we all know the meaning of moral discourse simply by being rational and knowing the language. The language of interpersonal relations is supposed to be obvious to all. But I ask, if that is so, why are there certain things which we do not say in front of the children? Obviously, because we are sure they will misunderstand. Children quickly learn how to use words, they can master the grammar and syntax all right, but they will require much more living before they master the meaning. The right to life debate simply assumes that everyone listening understands what "abortion" and "euthanasia" are. As if one could really know what these things are in the lived situation simply by looking them up in the dictionary. The fact of the matter is that most of the people to whom the right to life debate is directed do not really know what the partisans are talking about. And judging from the debates I have actually witnessed, I have a nagging suspicion that this may also be true for a large number of the debaters.

Lest this seem a minor difficulty, let me give an example. Another debate currently raging is over the advisability and even the possibility of fidelity—in marriage, in religious life, and in simple promise keeping. Can those who argue in favor of an absolute freedom which is incompatible with any sort of fidelity, and who live by that code, can they even begin to understand the meaning of the word "fidelity"? Obviously the fidelity debate is based on the same false assumption as the right to life debate.

Simply put, only a certain kind of person can understand the meaning of "abortion" and "euthanasia." And as I shall try to show a little later, it takes effort and discipline to become that kind of person. It is silly to think that those who make no effort in this regard and are undisciplined could possibly know what these things are, and presuming that one himself has become such a person it is quite absurd to enter into a *debate* with others who have not. With others who have, no debate is necessary.

A second false assumption which permeates the right to life debate is that men can change their basic values suddenly—as if upon hearing the arguments a person could do a 180° turn. That simply is not true. And the reason it is not true is that at any given moment we have become who we are because of our past. We have become a certain kind of person due to a long career involving our past relationships, decisions, cultural conditioning, etc. To suppose that something so laboriously built up can be altered suddenly by rational argument is to fly in the face of the facts. Even so-called sudden conversions on inspection yield a different picture in which the change was in the making for some time. In any event, if a rational argument has played any role it is not the decisive one in such cases. This is borne out in the contraception controversy of recent memory. Some Catholics anguished a long time before changing their consciences, but even those that apparently changed quickly report that the change was in the works for some time before it surfaced publicly.

If only a certain kind of person can understand abortion and euthanasia, and if it takes time to become such a one, then it is ridiculous to assume that you can produce such people suddenly by means of argumentation. To change someone's mind is the result, not the cause, of changing him. Since arguments result from the kind of person one already is, not the other way around, it is wrong-headed to think you can argue someone into being that way when already being that way is a major requisite for his really understanding your argument in the first place.

But a third questionable assumption actually makes it impossible for those who really understand abortion and euthanasia to be effectively heard in the debate. Because of the way we interpret the Western ideal of democracy in this country, we assume that a commitment to pluralism requires us to also hold that each man's voice is the equal of every other. When all voices are taken to be of equal quality we think we have democracy, but what we really have is a situation of anarchy. The anarchy which follows when no one can accept the leadership of another because no one can convince himself that his way of looking at matters is any better than one's own. Of course, as we have seen, the partisans in the right to life debate attempt to overcome this embarrassment of everyday American life by insisting that the voice of the experts (priests, theologians, philosophers, doctors, lawyers, sociologists and psychologists) is privileged and should be given more weight than other voices. But the inevitable anarchy sets in again, only this time on a higher level, as each of the experts in his turn finds it impossible to think that the view of any other expert is better than his own. Given such a view of pluralism, debates may be fun, and they may be effective as a means of keeping people off the streets at night, but they can't get anywhere.

The right to life debate is futile not only because it is based on a mistaken view of pluralism, but also because there is no respectable way to get the real expert in these matters into the debate. I am sick to death of listening to the debaters give their opinions and of having their credentials touted as sufficient reason for my accepting their position. I really don't care a fig about a person's medical, legal, theological or scientific *knowledge*. I am indifferent to the *position* or *office* he holds, be he president of a Right to Life Committee, Director of a Euthanasia Society, Head of Obstetrics, Chairman of the President's Commission on Population, Priest or Bishop. None of these things is germane to the matter before us. Life-death decisions are so important that they cannot safely be entrusted to any but the virtuous man. He and he alone is *the expert* in questions of abortion and euthanasia.

Let me clarify, since I am sure this position will receive criticism from every side. I do not mean to imply that I think that knowledge and expertise are unimportant in all the affairs of men; on the contrary, my entire life has been devoted to the attempt to acquire both. It is for that very reason that I refuse to be intimidated by the expertise of others on the life-death questions. I accept them as experts *in their fields;* it is just that in the field of the morality or goodness of abortion and euthanasia their voices are no longer expert unless they are in addition virtuous men. The value of what one has to say on abortion and euthanasia is not to be judged by a man's education or position, but rather on the basis of what kind of person he is. Yet in all the debates I have witnessed, no attempt is made to reveal that. It is simply ignored. And therefore I judge that I am at liberty to return the compliment by simply ignoring the whole debate. But to ignore the debate is not at all the same thing as to have no stand on abortion and euthanasia. To see why this is so, we will have to show just what it is about the virtuous man which gives him his special expertise in these matters.

The Real Expert: The Virtuous Man

The most important thing right from the start is to avoid getting into a debate over who is virtuous and who is not. It is more important at this point to determine what it is about virtuous men, as an identifiable group, which makes them special and the experts in life-death questions.

The virtuous man ought not to be distinguished from the rest of us because he does good acts and we do not, for on occasion we do. Nor is it the fact that he does them unfailingly and we always seem to vacillate. Besides we would then get into another debate about which acts were *really* good and, as you have observed by now, I have a strong aversion to debates. It is possible to describe the virtuous man without reference to any of his actions precisely because what is most significant about him is not his actions but the quality of his consciousness, his perspective on the world, his attitude toward reality. One is virtuous not primarily because of what one does, but because of what one is. *The virtuous man is in his person a special way of seeing the world.* His good acts follow from that vision. What makes the virtuous man the expert in life-death questions is precisely this fact—that he sees things which the rest of us do not. Why is that? How come he can see more than we can?

Freedom from Illusion. Seeing things as they really are is not as simple as is often supposed. In fact, one can safely say that if no special effort is made to see reality as it is rather than as we would like it to be, we shall very soon be able to see only our own illusions and fantasies. The ability of men to deceive themselves is boundless. We are indebted to Freud for discovering just how much the self is the source of fantastic illusions. I know of no illusion more fantastic than the one which currently has modern man by the throat and which has all but made the services of the virtuous man obsolete. I am speaking of the widely held opinion that there are no values other than those which men freely create themselves and conventionally agree to follow. That certainly is as titillating an illusion as any sexual fantasy and the full extent of its consequences is unimaginable. Interestingly enough, such an attitude, which is the exact opposite of that of the virtuous man, is presented as the height of human creativity and as indispensable if man is to be free. Nothing could be further from the truth. Man's freedom rests on the one freedom on which all the others depend—freedom from illusion. It is inconceivable that he could achieve authentic freedom by neglecting that on which it ultimately rests. Unless a man is free from self-delusions all else will be permeated with an inescapable unreality. To celebrate unreality is not freedom—it is insanity.

Now in order to be virtuous a man must possess that first freedom—freedom from illusion. It is the basis not only of all other freedoms, but also of virtue and goodness itself. The man who has it transcends the illusions to which he would otherwise fall prey, and hence more of what he sees is reality and less of it is merely a reflected self-image. Those of us without that freedom inevitably mistake the self for reality. This is what is meant by saying that the virtuous man is more selfless than the rest of us.

We are not talking now of that selflessness which marks our relations with other persons, but of that selflessness which must mark one's basic attitude toward reality if he is to see it as it is. Only the virtuous among us exhibit this basic selflessness toward reality, and therefore only they are really free to know reality. If we are sincere about solving the life-death questions correctly we have no alternative but to turn them over to such men.

I have a word for those who object to this position either because it is idealistic or because there are not enough really virtuous men. Even if there were not a single man of virtue on the face of the earth, it would not do to say that we should turn the life-death questions over to lesser men for solution. They not only could not solve the problem, they would be unable to even recognize that there was one. If in the name of hardheaded realism we have to admit that there are few or no virtuous men, this only means that no solution is readily available; it does not mean that what nonvirtuous men say should be accepted as doing justice to the reality of the situation. All that such men could possibly supply would be a doctored-up self-image which they then attempt to pass off as reality.

For those of the pro-Life[a] group who agree with what I have just said but conclude that it applies only to the members of the pro-Life[c] group and not to them, I also have a word. There is absolutely no substitute for virtue. Not religious belief, for it can and has all too often become fanatical and unreal. Nor absolute and unwavering adherence to principle, for reality may be calling for something else and because one is consistent but not virtuous he reads reality wrong and responds insensitively. Religious belief and adherence to principle when not coupled with authentic virtue can be as great a source of illusion as the self. Without virtue there is no way of being sure that obedience to religious commands and moral principles is identical with obedience to the demands of reality. In a word, religion without virtue is perhaps the cruelest illusion of them all—the illusion that to be religious *is* to be virtuous.

Obedience to Reality. Perhaps no word strikes more fear into the contemporary heart than the word "obedience." Yet it is really not so terrifying a word as all that. The objectivity of the scientist in his research is an acceptable example of obedience, even to liberals. Should the scientist manipulate and impose his view of things on reality, the results of his work would be scientifically worthless. Every scientist, indeed every real student, must have that kind of selfless openness to the reality he studies. If he does not, it will not reveal itself to him. The artist too, finds that he cannot have things all his own way. He must await his inspiration as a gift from reality, and once inspired he must accept the limitations which his materials and his craft impose on him. Artists don't create beauty. They discover it, and they often talk as if they were in the service of a higher power and are merely being obedient to it.

It is no different with the virtuous man. He cannot by means of dialectical skill, by long hours of study or argumentation, produce the good. That is not how it works. The vision of what should be done is given as a gift. The good reveals itself to the virtuous man because he adopts a patient, loving, honest and selfless attitude toward reality. He does not look at reality only as something out there to be grabbed and manipulated to better suit his interests and desires. But it takes real discipline to forego indulging one's illusions and serving one's own interests, and that is the price man must pay if he would see things as they really are.

It is not without significance, then, that modern man can accept the obedience required of the artist and scientist, but claims that the obedience of virtue contradicts his freedom. Science and art, while important, have to do only with a small portion of human life whereas virtue has to do with the overall quality of life and consciousness. As more comprehensive, it requires the greater discipline. Nothing interferes with the projects of the self like the demands of virtue. Nothing insures realism and destroys illusions as virtue does, and most of us find it much too hard to live realistically. To escape that fate we seek the comfort of our pet illusions and attempt to fashion the real to suit ourselves.

Now if this is the normal tactic of men, there is no reason to suppose that when it came to the abortion and euthanasia debates we would act any differently. Indeed the debate gives occasion for the men on both sides to attempt to shape reality in their own image. It promotes a rationalistic, acquistive and manipulating attitude toward reality, and as a technique is totally incompatible with the requirements of being virtuous.

I think it is not pure chance that the great men whom history paints as being truly virtuous were not inclined to exchange arguments with their adversaries. Socrates, who may be thought of as an exception, asked his questions in a very nonaggressive way in the hope that they might lead his fellowmen to "see" what he did. Until they really "saw," argument was useless; and once they did, it was unnecessary. It is no accident that there is something comic about trying to imagine Buddha, Jesus, Gandhi, or Pope John XXIII as parties to a debate. Yet we in the West have been sold a bill of goods that debate is the heart and soul of a pluralistic democracy. Small wonder then that Catholics in large numbers have flocked to the right to life debate as the best defense against the growing contemporary insensitivity to life. Little have they realized that such a move confers upon "reason" a task which only "virtue" can accomplish. Is there no other reasonable alternative left to those of us who are appalled at the way things are going?

If No Debate—What Then?

Obviously I think there is a debate. But it is by no means easy to map an alternate strategy. I am only encouraged to try because I find it difficult to conceive that anything I might suggest could be any more of a failure than the current right to life debate has been.

In order to offer a real choice the new strategy would certainly have to avoid at least the defects we have found to exist at the heart of the debate. But more specifically, it should : (1) Be able to promote and incorporate moral sentiment and virtue into the enterprise. (2) Be more responsive to the fact that men need time to grow in moral awareness and to change their lives, by offering them a way to engage in the mutual search necessary for such a change. (3) Avoid the arrogance and dogmatism of the past which has so effectively squelched that inquiry. And finally, (4) be comprehensive enough to deal not only with abortion and euthanasia but also with the contemporary climate which actually attempts to promote them as goods.

(1) *Promote Moral Sentiment and Virtue.* One of the things which we have traditionally looked to reason for is protection from our passions and emotions. Because they are just too chaotic to be reliable guides for human action, they must be kept under the constant control of reason. Now while there is great wisdom in such a posture if one considers only those passions which erupt suddenly like volcanoes, it fails as wisdom when one takes it to mean that all emotions are of that type. If I reject all emotions as untrustworthy, what am I to do with those noble sentiments which give life its human character? Must I reject those profound feelings with which we have been endowed to prevent our being heartless minds which work with the objectivity of a computer?

In our culture, until recently, little boys have been especially subjected to this view of things. Feeling deeply about things was reserved for the women; it was taken to be a sign of weakness in men. That left only reason as a reliable guide for conduct, but it was a reason which had lost its ability to feel deeply and hence one which had lost contact with much of what is most important in life. The detrimental effect of this sort of conditioning on our people can be seen by our inability as a nation to be sensitive (to feel anything) about what we have done to the poor and the aged in our midst. After years of downplaying the emotions as irrational what right have we now to complain about the insensitivity we see manifested toward the unborn and the terminally ill? But you can't engender human sensitivity into a people by arguing with them. That is why I feel that the debate tactic is itself so insensitive and hard-headed a response to our present needs.

If arguing won't do the job, what will? Only one thing—contact with other persons who are themselves sensitive to the humane dimensions of life. People who, despite the cultural pressures in the opposite direction, are sensitive to what reality reveals and who simply by being among us communicate that revelation. In short, contact with a truly virtuous man or woman. We increase our sensitivities by interpersonal contact with those who are more sensitive than we are.

(2) *Encourage Dialogue and Mutual Inquiry.* It is hard to imagine such contacts occurring in the context of a debate. Feelings often run quite high at such events, but they are not the kind of feelings which enhance the quality of our lives. Not every anger is just, but even just anger is not always an occasion for revelation. The urgency and the demand for immediate conversion so characteristic of the right to life debate turns the debaters into pitch-men, and makes such an event, when scheduled, appear for all the world like a traveling circus. By that I mean that debates are theatrical events held in public, and are ill-suited for the kind of personal contact and exchange which increases moral sensitivity. Dialogue is much better suited for that purpose.

Real dialogues usually occur when a few people gather in private in an atmosphere of trust and openness. No one seeks an advantage over the other, for they are engaged in a common task. To best the other in such a setting would be like trying to best yourself. Dialogues are permeated with a sense of patient expectation. No one rushes, no one demands immediate change in the other, for the common assumption of a dialogue is that we grow and mature but slowly. In such a setting the truly virtuous man comes into his own. For intimate contact with him soon reveals the unusually high quality of his vision; it becomes clear that he sees more than the rest and his voice is therefore valued more. Unable to make his worth known in the acrimonious context of a debate in which all the experts are telling everyone else what they should be doing, in a dialogue the virtuous man reveals the truth of things more by what he is than by what he says. Such a revelation orders no one around, forces no one, intimidates no one, it simply invites the others to be like the virtuous man, if they care to. Those who cynically say that very few will care to, simply underestimate the tremendous power of virtue. Do they actually think their arguments are stronger? Have they so soon forgotten the effect of Pope John on the world?

To those who say that there are few Pope Johns around, I would ask how they know that? How can you tell, unless you have had occasions for dialogue with them, how many of those who surround you are men and women of virtue? Unless you have had contact with someone in a dialogical situation, you really have no way of knowing whether his is the voice that will lead you all out of the darkness or not. Large assemblies have done little to help us escape the desert we are in. The time has come to pin our hopes on small groups.

A final word on dialogue. What I am endorsing here is the process or activity of dialoguing. I call for everyone interested in the quality of his life to be engaged in some way in this sort of activity on a regular basis. This should not be understood as a blanket endorsement of dialogue groups which are organized and more or less institutionalized. To say, "Every man in dialogue" is not at all the same thing as saying, "A dialogue group on every block." One engages in dialogue when and where he can. But it is easier than we think, for there are thousands of others who hunger for patient, respectful, growthful contact and exchange. It is just that we frighten them away when we always want to debate them or use them for our own purposes.

(3) *Avoid Dogmatism.* Nothing inhibits dialogue, betterment of moral sentiment and the cause of virtue more than dogmatism.

Dogmatic statements inevitably turn a dialogue into a debate. They attempt to engender moral sentiment by edict. And they get in the way of the silent and unspoken revelation of virtue. I do not insist that all dogmatic statements are false. Presumably it is only because one thinks they are true that one makes them. But even if they are true, I question the value of stating anything dogmatically. (That is why I am not a little bothered by having written this book.) There is nothing in the nature of truth which requires me to put it in dogmatic form. I may love my children very much, and could, if I wished, say so dogmatically. But it would be no less true if I chose some other way to communicate it. It is because men have chosen to say things dogmatically that we have dogmatic statements, but we are afraid to admit this fact and blame it on the nature of truth.

One reason for our choices is that we were taught to think that a truth once dogmatically stated became an absolute guide for human conduct. This certainly would make life a lot easier, but we are then faced with the problem of what to do with the exceptions which inevitably crop up. There are two accepted ways of handling the exceptions. We can either redefine our terms in the hopes of saving our dogmatic principle, or we can override the principle and make an exception in this one case. For example, if we say that it is always wrong to tell a lie, we will immediately be presented with the case in which by telling a lie to a Nazi soldier a man can save the Jew he has hidden in his attic. Now either we will redefine "lie" to exclude the telling of an untruth to someone under those special circumstances; or we will have to say that though it is generally wrong to lie, in this case it is all right. Whichever way we choose we will end up making an exception of a concrete case, thereby showing that the principle involved was not really an absolute after all. What this indicates is that the concrete situation determines the rules, not the other way around. Thus since dogmatic statements about human acts cannot really be absolute guides for conduct, I really see no reason to insist that we must use them. When one sees the terrible consequences which have followed their use throughout the centuries, it seems only intelligent to try as much as possible to live without them.

(4) *Treat the Problem Not Its Symptoms.* One cannot help being sympathetic toward all those in the debate who are battling so valiantly against liberalized abortion and euthanasia. They are like men coping with a bathtub that is overflowing but who are for some reason unable to turn off the water. They are condemned to be interminably mopping up. Of course, things might be a little wetter if they weren't on the job, but the water seems to be rising and they can never *solve* the problem. I have steadfastly refused to join the mopping up operation and have chosen instead to make some small effort at turning off the water, though I anticipate little thanks from those currently manning the mops.

The main problem is not abortion and euthanasia, it is that as a people we are no longer virtuous enough to see reality clearly, nor disciplined enough to cast off the illusions according to which life is currently led in the United States. We are an acquisitive people, ruled by the myths of commerce which know no limit to what can be manipulated for profit and self-interest. Now if the acquisitive mode prevails in every other sector of life, how can we expect it not to be present in the right to life controversy? To leave the other sectors of American life unchallenged, and to question the prevailing values only in cases of abortion and euthanasia is a bootless task. The right to life debate is marked by futility precisely because those who speak for the weak and helpless are asking their fellow Americans to exercise the kind of restraint with the unborn and terminally ill which is expected in no other area of American life. I consider such a position as idealistic and unrealistic as they undoubtedly will brand mine.

To solve the problem we must do no less than alter the mood of life in the United States. We must change the hearts and attitudes of men; until we do, none of us is safe from corruption. The only thing, leaving faith aside, powerful enough to accomplish this is the overwhelming attraction of the good. Since this is the only effective natural weapon we have, I thought it helpful to map a strategy for its use.

Conclusion

Undoubtedly many a reader will be disappointed at this point. After all, I have still not said what *I* think should be done in all those difficult abortion and euthanasia cases. To those who would ask me that question I have several things to say.

First, if I agreed to give a specific answer to your question I would be violating the very strategy I just proposed. It would only encourage argument and debate, not dialogue. I would be relying on a dogmatic statement rather than a lived experience and personal contact. And finally, I would be giving the impression that I thought I was a virtuous man. (The only virtue I lay claim to is that I am at least virtuous enough to "see" that only virtuous people have access to acceptable answers in life-death matters.)

Second, if I attempted to answer your question, I would give the impression that the answer can be found in some statement or other. The answer to agonizing life-death decisions is not to be found in what anyone *says*, but in what virtuous men *are*. If you are faced with a life-death decision and are still yourself virtuous enough to want to do the right thing, my only counsel to you is to seek out a person of greater virtue than yourself. If you are really interested in doing what is right, you should be able to recognize him. But once you do, don't pepper him with questions expecting immediate answers; be patient—we come to the truth but slowly. Dialogue with him, and by continued contact with him you will come to "see" the answer to your question.

Third, if you are unable to put yourself in contact with a person of greater virtue, you have no alternative but to rely on your own. You may think it meager, but whatever of it there is in you it is your *only* reliable contact with reality. All else is illusion and will certainly deceive you. By as much as you are able you must dispel the illusions, quiet your manipulative instincts and grate-fully accept the truth that will be revealed.

Fourth, I would counsel that you do not make the decision alone. It should be made in the company of those with whom you dialogue, taking advantage of whatever virtue they possess. You may want to prepare for that moment by having recourse to all the experts (priests, doctors, lawyers etc.), but the decision itself should be made in the company of those men and women with whom you are engaged in the serious search for what is right. Of course if you have no concern for doing right, any decision you make will be illusory.

I have a final word for those who laugh and scoff at all of this because they consider it abstract, naive, and the result of "ivory-tower thinking." A man's life and actions are fashioned as much by his ideals as by the realities of life. To rule out ideals and dreams as unrealistic is to ignore the natural power of good, and to forget that men cannot feel unmixed love for moral standards that are mediocre. The nobler thing tastes better to us, and that is all that can be said of it. When we reject an ideal and wound the good, when we suppress it because that is initially easier, we do not hear the end of it. As William James so wisely observed:

> The good which we have wounded returns to plague us with interminable crops of consequential damages, compunctions, and regrets. . . . It is the nature of these goods to be cruel to their rivals. They call out all the mercilessness in our disposi-tion, and do not easily forgive us if we are so softhearted as to shrink from sacrifice in their behalf.
>
> *The Writings of William James*, Modern Library,
> New York, 1968, pp. 626–27.

We have already begun to reap the consequences of our unwill-ingness to sacrifice for the lives of the weak and innocent. The call to virtue is certainly a call to an ideal, but the consequences of ignoring that call are all too real. It is in the light of the reality of those consequences that to sound the call to virtue is one of the most realistic things a man can do these days.

Part Two

WHAT A MODERN CATHOLIC BELIEVES ABOUT THE RIGHT TO LIFE

Chapter Five

ABORTION, EUTHANASIA AND THE FAITH COMMUNITY

THERE seems to be little if anything of faith in what has preceded. The arguments of the right to life debate are obviously the work of reason; and there does not seem to be anything particularly Catholic or Christian about the stand taken in the preceding chapter. On the other hand, there is nothing in Chapter Four which is against the faith either (unless the warning to avoid dogmatism is taken to be the equivalent of a warning against Catholicism and the church—which it is not). True, the virtuous man of whom I expect so much may be of any religious persuasion, or of no religious persuasion for that matter, but then the church has never taught that virtue could be found only among its members. Still the time has come to end this apparent religious neutrality if we are to live up to the title of this little book.

Some may say that it is high time, and complain about the fact that we have introduced the faith dimension so late in the game. Surely the whole book should have been devoted to the Catholic stand on abortion and euthanasia. I know this will sound strange, but from my point of view, it has been, and I am sure that those who promote abortion and euthanasia have had little trouble recognizing that fact. Why is it likely to elude so many Catholic readers?

First, because what I have said has not been presented in the form which is usually associated with Catholic treatments of abortion and euthanasia, or of anything else for that matter. "Catholic" presentations only recently have been getting away from the form which characterized them for so long. I am sure you remember it: It was doctrinal, dogmatic and authoritarian, based on such authorities as Scripture, the Pope, church councils and theological experts. For good measure it usually threw in a strong condemnation of the opposition.

Secondly, in matters of faith and morals there was a tone of righteousness and absolute certainty which marked the "Catholic" positions. If there is one thing which the church had, it was the answers. And since they were *the* answers those who accepted them in faith were blessed with a comfortable feeling of certainty.

And finally, though I have not rejected it, nowhere in what has gone before do I categorically endorse the traditional positions of the Catholic church on abortion and euthanasia. I have endorsed only the position which a virtuous man would take, and that is *not* the official position of the Catholic church. (There is something very strange about even being able to say that!)

Catholics have come to expect that form, that tone, and that conclusion, so when they find them all missing in what I have said up to now, they naturally conclude that there is nothing "Catholic" about it. And in all fairness, I didn't help things any by dividing the presentation into two parts, one involving what I *think*, the other involving what I *believe*. The truth of the matter is that what I think and what I believe are really two sides of the same coin. Let me explain.

I am of the opinion that the basic difference between traditional and modern Catholics, the thing that separates them theologically although they remain, hopefully, brothers in the faith, is the way each views experience and the role of the church among men. Only the modern Catholic will immediately see the faith dimensions of what I had to say about the virtuous man.

Experience as Revelatory

Traditional Catholicism is authoritarian and so concerned with orthodoxy that it has little or no use for "human experience." One educated as we were got no indication that Christianity had anything whatsoever to do with experience. The revealed Scriptures, the infallibility of the popes, and the absolute orthodoxy of one's teachers made personal experience practically superfluous. Being a Catholic in the old sense meant complete assurance of the truth or orthodoxy of doctrines simply on the say-so of divine or ecclesiastical authority *without recourse to experience.*

One reason traditional Catholicism ignored experience was its limited view of "revelation." Revelation according to traditional teaching ended with the death of the last of the apostles, and not even the infallible pope could add to it substantially. All who come after the apostles could only draw out what was originally revealed. This meant that Catholics were a people living in the past, and when their present experiences seemed to contradict what their teachers taught had been revealed, they felt obliged to ignore their experiences. I personally find it difficult to base my faith on the experience of someone else, no matter what his credentials. Doing that tends to produce a faith which is all too easily challenged by new experiences. Yet, unless I err, this is precisely what we have mistakenly thought we were being asked to do as Catholics. We have tended to look to the Old Testament, to the New Testament, to the theological authorities of the past and to a long list of infallible Popes for the meaning of our faith, and have overlooked the obvious importance of present experience. This is a great mistake, and a serious misunderstanding of what it means to be a Catholic.

The reason is obvious: Revelation is *not* over; *God is constantly revealing himself to us in our experience.* The man of faith cannot ignore experience because the doctrines of faith have made it unnecessary. Rather he truly needs experience because it is there that much, though not all, of what is true in faith is available for the "seeing." Faith is not primarily a way of seeing things which lie beyond the world of experience. Faith, like virtue, is a way of truly seeing the reality delivered in human experience, and like virtue it confers the power of responding in ways that are sensitive to, not manipulative of, what is revealed.

Experience Reveals the Presence of Evil. One does not have to live very long before he runs into the perversity of evil in human life. These days we tend to explain it in terms of heredity and environment. Man, we are told, is basically good, and whatever corruption there is in his behavior is due either to his genes, his psychological make-up, or to the negative influence of society. To explain evil in this way eliminates the man of faith and the man of virtue as serious sources of insight into the problem. Instead we find ourselves looking for "salvation from evil" to the biologists, psychologists and sociologists. We should look to these experts for help in all those instances of evil which arise from sources beyond the control of the individual. But what if, in addition to these, man is not basically good; what if he has an inherent propensity for evil? That he does is one of the indisputable facts of experience. And to establish that we need not look at others, we have but to look honestly into our own hearts. The good that we would do we leave undone, the evil that we would leave undone, we do. This is not only a doctrine of faith (original sin), it is a fact of experience. Only our illusions keep us from recognizing that we are a fallen race and a wounded people.

Experience Reveals the Gift Dimension of Life. If that were all that experience revealed, there would be little reason to hope. But despite our predicament we do have reason to hope, because each man also experiences within himself the graciousness of existence. The most precious things in life cannot be produced by human ingenuity, nor merited by personal effort; they can only be gratefully accepted as gifts. A profound gratuity marks the innermost recesses of what is human. Experience soon teaches us that friendship, love, community, freedom, hope and all the most important things in life are always gifts.

Yes, even freedom is a gift. For because we are wounded and fallen, we cannot be sure that when invited to respond openly and generously to others we will be free enough to do it. We find a hundred reasons and arguments (remember the right to life debate) why we should not. Sometimes we find that we can respond but we know that the power to do so was a gift, and we cannot be sure that we will be able to respond the same way tomorrow. The freedom and power to do what love requires is not something over which we have complete control. Sometimes we have it, and sometimes we don't.

We might be able to persuade ourselves that we receive these gifts from other people, but upon reflection this does not prove to be a totally satisfactory explanation. We may feel that we have received much from others, especially from the men and women of faith and virtue in our lives, but what we receive from them is not theirs by right. That is, they too possess it as gift, not by their own efforts and strength. The gift dimension of life cannot be reduced to the human. Experience directly reveals a world overflowing with gifts, but we have no such direct experience of their ultimate giver. Yet we know that there can be no gifts without a giver, and gifts in abundance there surely are. Once again, this is not only a doctrine of faith (that mankind is graced), it is an evident dimension of life to which only our acquisitive culture blinds us.

Perhaps now it is a little clearer why I feel that what I think and what I believe are but two sides of the same coin. Up to this point at least, the man of virtue and the man of faith are "seeing" the same things. It is only when we take the next step that faith takes us beyond what the virtuous man as such can see. It has to do with the question: "What say you of Jesus of Nazareth?" To that, a man of virtue would probably respond by saying that he was one of the noblest, one of the most inspiring and one of the most virtuous of men. (Who could quarrel with that?) Which would cause the man of faith to ask: "Is that all?" To which the man of virtue would reply: "What more is there?" Nothing shows better than this exchange the gulf that divides them. But though the man of faith and the man of virtue may differ on such questions as whether Christ is God-Incarnate, or what is the role of the church, it is my contention that they would absolutely agree when it came to the life-death questions. When it comes to handling abortion and euthanasia there is nothing to choose between the man of real virtue and the real man of faith. Put another way, while it is possible for them to disagree on something which only one of them "sees," it is inconceivable that what they both "see" would not agree. This accounts for my conviction that this entire book has been devoted to the "Catholic" position on abortion and euthanasia.

The Role of Church

Because modern and traditional Catholics differ about the role of experience in their religious lives, it is not surprising that they also differ on the role of their church among men. For too long it was thought that the only orthodox view was to see the church as the source of salvation to men, as an infallible repository of doctrinal truth, and *the* authoritative voice in matters of morals. Those who continue to see the church in this light are acting in accord with their faith then when they try to have that voice heard and followed in the right to life debate. Since that is how they view things, they have no real alternative. The only reason that I did have an alternative is because I have a far different view of the mission of the church. Given that view, I had no alternative but to refuse to participate in the debate. Each side is acting in accord with its faith and is above criticism on that point.

As for the question, "What say you of Jesus of Nazareth?," in faith I say this: He is the full embodiment of the graciousness of existence. He is God's gift of himself to the world. In his humanity he experienced the gift dimension of human existence as we all do; but in his person he is God's graciousness to man become visible and incarnate. Jesus is "Gift" with a capital "G," and as such he gives all wounded men reason to hope.

Now Jesus couldn't epitomize the absolute graciousness of God toward man if he were to give it only a conditional expression. If the Incarnation means that we shall be graced by God only on the condition that we do this or that, then with the Herod of *Jesus Christ Superstar* we would be justified in saying to Jesus: "You're not the Lord—you're nothing but a fraud!" To be Lord is both *to be* and *to announce* to the world the unconditional gratuity of God toward men. Because we live in a conditional world, we find that difficult, if not impossible to believe. To our limited minds it is easier to think of God as setting conditions on his love and generosity. If we do this, then he'll do that. And what is more, once we fulfill those imaginary conditions of ours, we then claim by right to have earned that which can only be freely and unconditionally given and received. The coming of Christ into our world was precisely to make that impossible thing believable to men.

If that is the context of Christ's coming, then his founding of the church must be seen in that same light. It simply will not do to paint a picture of the church which violates the revelation which Jesus is. Unfortunately, the Catholic religion has in many of its practices forgotten to give witness to divine graciousness. All too often it dispenses the spiritual goods which have been gifts to it, with anything but graciousness. Conditions are set on almost every good the church dispenses, some of them harsh and unfeeling. One cannot help being reminded of the unforgiving steward who when he was graciously dispensed from his large debt by his master, turned around and put those of his fellow stewards who owed him a pittance in jail (Cf. Matt. 18:23–35).

It has taken far too long for Catholics finally to ask themselves why it is that God's world is marked with an unconditional gratuity, while his church isn't. But once they do, they are on the way to giving up being traditional and to joining the ever growing numbers of modern Catholics.

You see a modern Catholic has finally learned the most fundamental lesson of life and of his faith: The unutterably wonderful fact that there are no obligations of a religious nature since *the whole religious enterprise is from start to finish a gratuity.* Christ did not come so that God could give himself to men, nor that gifts of salvation and forgiveness could be given. All these things were already given from the start; mankind has never been without them. *Christ came to give men hope by making the literally unbelievable extent of divine generosity publicly visible.* And since the church is the continuation of Christ's presence among men, it is only logical to conclude that this is her main mission as well.

In view of her mission to give men a sign of hope, it no longer seems relevant to say that the church alone is the source of salvation, since God offers that to all without discrimination. And the keys of forgiveness given to Peter do not indicate that the church of Rome has the concession on such a spiritual benefit; the keys are rather a public sign that forgiveness is available to *all*, and that to lay hold of that gift they need only want to. Finally, if the church is the repository of infallible truth, it is not because it has all the correct answers to life's moral questions, but rather because it is to be the living proof of the totally unimaginable truth about God's absolute and unqualified generosity to man. An infallibility which failed to safeguard that truth would be most obviously fallible.

Called to be a sign of hope to the world, the Catholic community is, at present, itself a scandal of hopelessness from the Chair of Peter down to the least of the brethren. Do the bishops, cardinals, and pope appear to be happy, hopeful men? Do the pastors and the priests exude the confidence of those who trust in the boundless generosity of God? Do laymen face the future with promise? Obviously, something seems to have gone wrong.

Form Me A People. On every side we hear the complaints: Abortion mills are springing up all over; growing numbers of young people are engaged in an orgy of drugs and sex; the aged are treated shamefully and are now faced with our ultimate rejection of them—euthanasia. To stem the tide of this collective insanity, many Christians have entered the right to life debates, but they don't exactly give one the impression of hopefulness either. The Gospel picture of the Lord is not of one who acted as we Catholics do today, yet this world was not so different from our own. In those days the collective insanity was the Roman Empire, but Christ did not shout the dogmas of institutionalized religion at it. Nor did he spend his time railing against the rampant immorality of his day. His anger was directed not against the immoral of his time, but against the professional religionists and moralists (Pharisees) of the day. With but few exceptions, like feeding the multitudes who had followed him, he engaged in no social work. What he did do was to seek out his fellow men and speak his "Word" to them. A "Word" which was revelation, judgment and invitation to those that heard it and began to "see" things in a new light.

Amid the immorality of his day, Jesus went on about his Father's business of forming an identifiable group (church) who by their lives would give witness to the infallible truth of divine generosity, thereby giving their contemporaries reason to hope. Today our task is just the same. We are not to go around declaiming every evil, telling other people what to do and accusing them of breaking the law. We are not to preach the law of God to others, we are to so live it in public that our fellows will be unable to miss its significance. *To give our brothers hope we are to live the future now—in faith.* That future is the one foretold by St. John in the Apocalypse. He foresees a time when men will be free of their illusions, when they will no longer be acquisitive and self-serving, when each man will be at peace with every other, and all men will be so at one with one another that the present God of mystery shall choose to dwell fully and openly with them.

But our fellow Americans are a hardheaded, practical bunch who put little store in ideals and utopian schemes; after all, they are nobody's fools. If we expect such men to take hope and to "see" things differently, we must be free of our own illusions *now*. We must cease being acquisitive and self-serving in our dealings with others *now*. We must truly be at peace with one another and respectful of one another's lives *now*. We must exhibit the marvelous freedom of men who follow the law of love so that God may truly dwell among us obviously and no longer in mystery—*even now*. God's generosity with us is reason enough for us to be hopeful, but how can men come to know this important religious truth? Only by observing it in the concrete, by actually coming into contact and exchange with a faith community which itself is living proof of the unwarranted, unpredictable, boundless generosity of the Lord. And wherever in the Lord's name you find such a group—there you have church.

Abortion and Church

I know of no act which is more out of keeping with the nature of church than abortion. By as much as a faith community opens itself up to abortion, by that much it ceases to be church. This is not to pass judgment on any particular cases, since I continue to be reluctant to do that. But I think it should be clear that if one holds that the church is an identifiable people which is to publicly witness and celebrate divine graciousness to man, the taking of prenatal life *at any stage* of its development is a fundamental rejection of the gift-dimension of human life in the name of some other value one holds more dear. But to hold some other value more dear is freely to separate oneself from that community I have called church. Abortion is the epitome of un-church, and is by nature incompatible with the mission of the Christian community.

But that is not all, more can be said. There is one particular kind of abortion which deserves special mention because of the added incompatibility with church which it embodies. I am speaking of those abortions which are purely whimsical, or which are justified on the basis that it is strictly a private matter and nobody else's business. As an example of a "whimsical abortion" I cite the following.

It was recently reported in the press that a woman had her unborn tested for phenylketonuria, a major cause of retardation. The testing has advanced to such a stage that now it is possible for the fetologist to determine the sex of the unborn as well as its health status. The physician informed the woman, with great enthusiasm, of the perfect health of her baby and in passing mentioned its sex. To his consternation, the woman informed him that she and her husband really wanted a child but one of the opposite sex. She confided her intention to have the healthy fetus aborted. Fetologists are talking now of withholding information regarding the sex of the unborn; others are suggesting a law suit to force them to divulge everything they know even when they are sure such information will be used against the life of their patient—the fetus.

It is hard to imagine a more calloused posture toward the gratuity of life. But more than that, such cases indicate another attitude which is totally destructive of church. Church is an identifiable people, not a person. To be a member of a people, in the sense we have been using it, means that I have some regard for the others who with me make up a people committed to celebrating the gratuity of life. Whenever one's commitment to his own freedom is such that it precludes those others with whom he is joined in community, actions performed with that motivation rend the fabric of the group. "Whimsical abortions" not only throw the gift of life back in the face of reality, they do so from an attitude which in principle is destructive of community. Such abortions reject the importance of respecting the gratuity of life the faith community is committed to celebrate, and they consider being "person" more important than being part of a witnessing "people." They are unchristian then on two counts. This does not imply that Christians are unaware of the importance of becoming a person. It is just that they know that one cannot successfully become a person except in the presence and with the help of one's fellows.

None of this should be taken to mean that the members of the faith community will never be presented with agonizing situations in which abortion seems to be an apparent solution. What I have said does mean that abortion should and need never occur among Christians. I think that point can be graphically put this way. Suppose for a moment that the gestation period in humans were 9 days and not 9 months. What would our attitude toward abortion be under such circumstances? It seems to be that in all but the life-against-life case, we would counsel the woman to bring the child to term. And we would promise to aid her in any and every way we could, even to the point of taking a child she felt incapable or unwilling to raise. The child could then be placed with a couple who wanted it and were willing to raise it. The point is clear; we are unwilling to do for 270 days what common sense would dictate as reasonable if it were done only for 9 days. What I am suggesting is that a truly Christian community would be made up of persons who refused to allow time to be the deciding factor when it came to the gratuity of life. If others would do whatever had to be done for 9 days, Christians should be willing to do it for as long as necessary.

The pro-abortion people delight in presenting us with desperate cases insisting that the only source of hope in those situations is an abortion. It is just the reverse with a faith community that is really church. They know, through faith, that such a view is illusory and that because abortion is a fundamental denial of the graced character of human life, it not only can't be the source of any substantial hope but can only lead to an ever more pervasive hopelessness.

Euthanasia and Church

Euthanasia is not so absolutely opposed to church, as we have defined it, as is abortion. This is because to relieve the sufferings of the terminally ill in their last extremity can often appear as a great and beneficent gift. This seems to be in accord with the moral sentiments of the average man. However, I think we are still able to use our "gratuity principle" to see things a bit more clearly.

What makes euthanasia appear so ambiguous is the cultural climate in which people in our country must now face death. Once one has been declared terminally ill, no one wants to have anything to do with him. Whether it is because we shrink from observing the sufferings of others, or whether it is because we are afraid that those sufferings will make some demand on us matters little. The effect is the same—the terrible isolation of the terminally ill precisely at the time when they desire and would benefit most from contact and exchange with their fellows. While it may be natural for us to flee from death (our own), we avoid death at all costs, even the deaths of others. This is hardly a humane policy, and it has nothing to recommend it as far as the faith community is concerned. Some have already seen this, and there are now many experiments going on in which whole hospitals are devoted exclusively to the dying.

One such is St. Christopher Hospital in London, England. It admits only the terminally ill. The patient, his doctor and his family must all be aware of the hopelessness of the case if the patient is to be admitted. Upon entering the hospital, the patient knows that no medical procedures will be performed to prolong his life, and he will receive medicine in doses geared only to ease his pain. What could be more hopeless, you may ask. It conjures up images of the old elephant seeking out the elephants' graveyard in his last extremity. Would it not give those who run from death whenever it occurs a good excuse for removing the dying from sight? And once out of sight, out of mind.

Interestingly enough, it has not worked out that way at all. The results have been illuminating. St. Christopher's is one of the happiest of places. The patients are given only minimal medical treatment, but they have access to spiritual consolation, the companionship of others, and they are given opportunities, by as much as they are able, to do the things they never had time for before. One patient, a 72-year-old woman dying of cancer, recently started to learn German. There is no limit to visiting hours at St. Christopher's and the place is quite often overrun with happy children. The staff of the hospital, having been freed from expending their energies in hopeless procedures and from trying to maintain a subterfuge with the patients, report that they have been able to devote their efforts exclusively to helping their patients die well. This is real euthanasia, and it is fully compatible with the demands of Christianity. In such a setting direct euthanasia seems to be completely out of place.

The reason we are experiencing an increased demand for direct euthanasia in this country is because we are unwilling to make the kinds of commitments which would insure for the dying the chance to die in dignity and to celebrate life's graciousness themselves right up to the end. As with abortion, we put forth euthanasia not as the best solution to the problem, but as the only solution to the problem, which makes no further demands on us. But a real faith community would be made up of those whose commitment to the gratuity of life makes them willing to be imposed on. They would celebrate the graciousness of life right up to the end—and beyond. And it is hoped that upon seeing their witness, others would join the party (in both senses of the word).

The Answer Is Itself Gift

It is funny that no matter how much things change, they somehow stay the same. The discussions of abortion and euthanasia among Catholics today have a familiar ring to them and remind one of those discussions which today's adults held about necking, petting and "making out" when they were young. The question was always: "How far can I go? How far can I arouse her with my passionate kissing before it is a mortal sin?" "How far can I go, Father, in getting him to kiss me good night before I am seducing him?" And so it went. Today the questions are really the same, it is just that the stakes are higher. "Could I abort if he raped me?" "Is it all right to abort? You see, I'm not married." "We didn't want a child just yet; you see John just lost his job and so we've got to abort. You understand don't you?" And so it goes.

These questions are alike not only because each seeks to find out where the limit on human desires is to be placed, but also because each of them is in a very real sense a nonquestion. They are nonquestions because the one asking them usually already knows the answer. I have been at some pains throughout this little book to suggest that the kind of "knowing" involved here has little to do with arguments and reasonings and that it is more like insight, vision, or revelation; it is given as a gift, not acquired by study. But precisely because such knowledge is gift; it can be refused and rejected, and we go on innocently asking questions as if from ignorance.

But we adults who have lived and experienced life are neither innocent nor ignorant. We feign these postures, and because we do, our questions condemn us. Even if we really didn't know the answers, we who have tasted so much of life would still have no right to be ignorant. And because we really do know the answers, we obviously have no right to feign ignorance. The young and inexperienced deserve better from us. We do them no service when we allow the impression to be given that there really is a basis for the current controversy about abortion and euthanasia. But we cannot ask them to be open to the graciousness of life when treating the unborn and the terminally ill if we have ourselves rejected the gift of life's vision and have failed to share it with them.

NOTES

Chapter One

1. This aspect of dialogue was put very well by Rev. J. Donald Monan, S.J., in his address to the Vocation Directors of America in September of 1966 when he said: "One who enters a dialogue at ten o'clock, if it is truly an historical dialogue, does not know what responses he will be making at noon. Nor, unless it is a debate or a seduction, does it set out to wrest certain admission from its partner."

2. Cf. Reuel L. Howe, *The Miracle of Dialogue*, Seabury Press, N.Y., 1963, p. 84.

3. Since I consider the debate on the right to life to be by nature endless, it will be understood why I make no attempt to bring it to a final conclusion. However, this should not be taken to mean that the situation is hopeless, for one is always at liberty to simply stop debating. But more of that later. As a model of mastery of the choreography regarding the abortion debate see: Daniel Callahan, *Abortion: Law, Choice and Morality*, Macmillan, N.Y., 1970.

4. Cf. Roger Wertheimer, "Understanding the Abortion Argument," *Philosophy and Public Affairs*, Fall 1971, Vol. I, 1, p. 85.

5. Cf. Jean Francois Revel, *Without Marx and Jesus*, Delta Book, Dell Publishing, N.Y., 1972, pp. 153–181.

6. Catholics participating in the right to life debate have been particularly hampered and frustrated by this provision of public discussion. No matter how scrupulous they are in respecting the pluralistic mood of the public forum, they are accused of violating it simply because they are Catholic. The logical consequence of that kind of thinking is the eventual barring from public discussion of all men and women of religious conviction (a consequence hardly in accord with our commitment to pluralism). While this is truly unfortunate, it is a logical consequence of the conduct which has characterized Catholic participation in the public forum in the past. Our former sins have come home to roost.

7. The fact that human life is organic and that there has been a virtual revolution in biological and medical knowledge due to recent advances, is reason enough to avoid any stand on the right to life issue which would be incompatible with those advances. It would be immediately rejected as naive. Aware of this, both sides attempt to give their audiences short courses in the new biology and the new medicine.

The current debate is also sensitive to the fact that there have been comparable advances in human or social sciences. If one wants to successfully participate in the right to life debate, he had better take seriously the most current findings of psychologists, sociologists, demographers, and experts on urbanization and the human environment. One of the surest ways to prove one's seriousness in this regard is to show some virtuosity in the handling of the statistics and computer findings which permeate these disciplines. Each side seems to have no trouble finding ways and means to use the statistics to its own advantage.

Since the context of the current debate is the growing dissatisfaction among our people with the traditional laws regarding abortion and euthanasia, it is impossible to avoid the legal precedents and consequences attached to any right to life stand. Some claim that to change the existing laws requires a constitutional amendment because it would in some instances involve the taking of a human life without the due process guaranteed by our Constitution.

8. It is very important to point out here that the so-called evidence from experts is of a factual sort and is not sufficient to settle the right to life debate, which is a disagreement on how we are to value and interpret the facts. Or to put the matter another way, if that on which the disagreement turns were simply another fact, there would be no debate on the matter (just as we would not think of debating about batting averages); we would simply ask the experts to determine the facts for us. This should be somewhat consoling, for it means that one need not himself be an expert to take a stand on the right to life. (Even when the experts take a stand, their position goes beyond the realm of their expertise—though they are very reluctant to admit that.) Then too, as I hope to show, it is possible to take a stand on the right to life all the while refusing for good reasons to take part in the debate.

9. This is particularly difficult for all members of the right to life debate because they are committed to particular partisan positions. They try to surmount the difficulty by claiming that the partisan position they espouse is really the one our ideal man would follow. This claim is not always taken seriously, however, especially in the case of men and women of religious commitment. They are always being accused of violating the ideal of rationality no matter what they actually say. They return the favor, however, by showing that those who are for abortion and euthanasia are also guilty of special pleading. So each pleads his special case, all the while proclaiming to the world that he is simply giving expression to what any truly rational man would hold. Obviously even so serious an endeavor as the right to life debate is not without its comic aspects.

10. Present day proponents of Principle I are quick to point out that such situations of lives in mortal conflict need not occur because of the advances of medicine. They seem to say then that the life-against-life case is no longer relevant to the debate. This can hardly be true. For the one thing that principles of human action are supposed to do is cover all cases both actual and hypothetical. If a principle cannot handle hypothetical cases, it will soon be judged inadequate according to the norms of rationality. The opponents of Principle I are well aware of this and keep pressing hypothetical cases against it.

11. Even in these extreme cases, the motivating force in favor of intervention is an almost absolute stand on the inviolability of innocent human

life. (In the case of the truck driver, it might be thought that the bullet violates his life less than the fire would.) While less rigid than the position based on Principle I, it is misleading to call the one based on Principle II a liberal stance.

Chapter Two

1. On the importance of the advances in genetics in the abortion debate see: Paul Ramsey, "Points in Deciding About Abortion" in John T. Noonan, *The Morality of Abortion,* Harvard U. Press, 1970, pp. 64–68; Daniel Callahan, *Abortion: Law, Choice and Morality,* Macmillan, 1970, pp. 378–383.

2. But, of course, the argument does go on. This can only be for one of two reasons. Either Argument #1 is not valid and true, or else despite intrinsic worth it does not strike the audience as conclusive. I suspect that it is the latter for reasons which will be obvious later.

3. Cf. David W. Louisell, "Abortion, the Practice of Medicine and the Due Process of Law," *UCLA Law Review,* Vol. 16, 1969. David W. Louisell and John T. Noonan, Jr., "Constitutional Balance" in John T. Noonan, Jr., ed., *The Morality of Abortion,* Harvard University Press, 1970, pp. 220–260.

4. Patrick Devlin, *The Enforcement of Morals,* Oxford University Press, 1965. H.L.A. Hart, *Law, Liberty, Morality,* Vintage Book, Random House, N.Y. Cf. Daniel Callahan, *op. cit.,* Ch. XIII "Abortion on Request and Legal Reform," pp. 448–483. Paul Marx, O.S.B., *The Death Peddlers,* St. John University Press, Collegeville, 1971, pp. 64–106. Alan Guttmacher, *The Case for Legalized Abortion Now,* Berkeley, Diablo Press, 1967.

5. It therefore came as no surprise to me that four days after I completed this little book, the Supreme Court of the United States announced its decision in the Georgia case and all but struck down the anti-abortion laws of the States. Many engaged in the right to life debate had never seriously considered such a decision as a possibility, and so they were confident that the long legal tradition of respect for prenatal life would have to go on uninterrupted. It now appears that this is not to be the case.

By adopting the arguments of a woman's unilateral right to privacy and to control her body, the Supreme Court has sided with the proponents of the rebuttal to Argument #2. The matter will obviously not end there since the dissenting Justices sided with the proponents of Argument #2. There will be continued activity on both sides of the debate just as there was before, but from now on the law will favor the pro-Life[c] groups rather than the pro-Life[a] groups.

Many will claim now that the matter is strictly a private one and that the pro-Life[a] groups will have to use powers of moral persuasion to achieve their goals and can no longer depend on the State for support. As I have repeatedly said, this will not really work in a society such as ours where the commitment to pluralism embodies the assumption that each man's voice is the equal of every other man's voice. On that point see: Ch. 4 below.

6. There is no necessary advantage in having many absolute or near-

absolute principles. But when you do have more than one, it is necessary to impose an order of priority on them. The question which remains unanswered is what relationship the sovereignty of conscience, the right to control one's body and the right to sexual freedom have to the right to life. Are they all of equal value? When they come into conflict how does one adjudicate the claims of each? Obviously this accounts for the greater complexity of the pro-Life[c] case as compared to the more simple and straightforward pro-Life[a] case. But complexity may or may not have bearing on the conclusiveness of one's reasonings.

7. For a most cogent presentation of Argument #4, Cf. Judith Jarvis Thomson, "A Defense of Abortion," *Philosophy and Public Affairs*, Vol. I, No. 1, Fall 1971, pp. 47ff.

8. On the various rights and interests involved in the conception of new life, Cf. George Huntston Williams, "The Sacred Condominium" in John T. Noonan, *op. cit.*, pp. 146–171.

9. Cf. David W. Louisell and John T. Noonan, Jr., "Constitutional Balance" in John T. Noonan, *op. cit.*, pp. 220–260.

10. Of course, the rub in a pluralistic society is that there is no agreement on just what is moral and what is not. Still, in order to protect society from any and every fanaticism, it must be understood that the right to conscience is the right to be moral. That will certainly rule out recourse to the right of conscience in order to condone acts which are obviously immoral in the eyes of all, e.g., wanton cruelty, murder, rape, etc. When there is disagreement about the morality of an act, as is the case with abortion, it is still incumbent on both sides of the debate to realize that the right to conscience is a "moral" category, not merely a social or political one.

11. They are empty not because they have no intellectual or moral value for those who can understand them, but rather because they fail to touch the average man or woman where he lives. Men simply do not generally reason their way to profound life-death decisions. They rely more on "gut reactions," and it is simply false to assert that such guides are always misleading.

It is usually within the context of the life-against-life discussion that Catholic thinkers have traditionally employed the famous principle of double effect. However important it may be in the order of moral theory, it remains an empty formalism for most. I avoided using the double-effect argument in the rebuttal to Argument #7, because it is presently being challenged and much debated in its own right and it would have been impossible to do it justice. I deemed it better to refer the interested reader to some of the items included in the ever growing literature on the subject. On the principle of double effect see: Daniel Callahan, *op. cit.*, pp. 422–426; Thomas Aquinas, *Summa Theologica*, II–II, 64, 7; Paul Ramsey, "The Morality of Abortion" in James Rachels, *Moral Problems*, Harper & Row, 1971, pp. 16–27; Philippa Foot, "The Problem of Abortion and the Doctrine of the Double Effect" in Rachels, *op. cit.*, pp. 28–41; John Dedek, *Human Life*, Sheed and Ward, 1972, pp. 21–32; Bruno Schüller, S.J., "What Ethical

Principles are Universally Valid," *Theology Digest,* XIX (1971), pp. 23–28 and *Theological Studies,* 32 (1971), pp. 80–97.

12. Speaking quite technically, the first three are generally taken to be means of "conception control," and only abortion is truly "birth control." There is some dispute among the experts as to whether some of the chemical contraceptives are not actually abortifacients. If it turns out that some of them are, this will not add to the list of ways of curtailing fecundity. Rather it will mean that some of the items listed as chemical contraceptives are really chemical agents for inducing abortion and should be listed under (4) rather than (2).

13. For more hearty souls I recommend: Paul Erlich and Richard Harriman, *How to Be a Survivor,* Ballantine, N.Y., 1971; Paul Erlich, *The Population Bomb,* Ballantine Books, N.Y., 1968; Garrett Hardin, *Population, Evolution and Birth Control: A Collage of Controversial Readings,* W. H. Freeman and Co., San Francisco, 1969; and by the same author "Parenthood: Right or Privilege?," *Science,* 169 (1970), p. 427 and "The Tragedy of the Commons," *Science,* 162 (1968), pp. 1243–1248; Anthony Burgess, *The Wanting Seed,* Ballantine, N.Y., 1970; Daniel Callahan, *The American Population Debate,* Doubleday, N.Y., 1971; Barry Commoner, *The Closing Circle,* Bantam Book, N.Y., 1972; Barry Commoner, *Science and Survival,* Ballantine, N.Y., 1970.

14. *The Terrible Choice: The Abortion Dilemma,* Bantam Books, N.Y., 1968, in Foreword by Pearl S. Buck, p. xi.

15. Cited in: Dr. and Mrs. J. C. Wilke, *Handbook on Abortion,* Hiltz Publishing Co., Cincinnati, 1971, p. 81.

16. I don't mean to suggest that the reader cannot have made an evaluation of the ten arguments presented in this chapter, and decided either for or against abortion. I merely affirm that any decision made on the matter is not simply a function of rationality. Something besides rationality determined which of the arguments you *preferred.* It is that something else which we shall consider in Ch. 4.

Chapter Three

1. The "wedge argument" is that a breakdown in the protection traditionally afforded life in one area leads to a breakdown of the protection of life in all areas. To liberalize the abortion laws will inevitably lead to a threat to the lives of the aged, the retarded and the terminally ill. It is difficult if not impossible to show any *necessary* connection between abortion and euthanasia. Cf. Cecilia Bok, "The Wedge—Not So Simple," *Hastings Center Report,* Dec., 1971. But whatever connection there is would seem to run in the opposite direction. There is a stronger natural sentiment in favor of euthanasia than for abortion. This indicates that the ordinary man has little trouble in making a decisive distinction between them and that to be for the one does not require a man to be for the other as well. Of course, some are for both simply because they are anti-establishment, but then we are no longer concerned with the "right to life" debate.

2. For that display of impeccable logic we are indebted to: Austin Fagothey, *Right and Reason,* C. V. Mosley, St. Louis, 1963, 3rd edition, p. 240.

3. Cf. John Dedek, *Human Life,* Sheed and Ward, 1972, p. 127.

4. Cf. Norman St. John-Stevas, *The Right to Life,* Holt, Rinehart and Winston, 1963, Chapter 3, "A Right to Die," pp. 36–54. Chapter 4, "A Right to Kill Oneself," pp. 55–79, is an excellent brief account of the history of attitudes in England and the United States on suicide in its non-euthanasia senses.

5. Karl Barth, *Church Dogmatics,* Vol. III, 4, T. and T. Clark, Edinburgh, 1961, p. 427.

6. Cf. C. E. Pappworth, *Human Guinea Pigs: Experimentation on Man,* Beacon Press, Boston, 1968.

7. Gerald Kelly, S.J., *Medico-Moral Problems,* Catholic Hospital Association, St. Louis, 1958, p. 129.

8. Many accept this as a quite natural attitude and cite approvingly the practice among the Eskimo of encouraging suicide for the aged who have become a burden on society. Since Eskimo society was always in a survival crisis due to the harsh conditions under which they lived, this can be seen as just one more harsh reality with which they were forced to live, i.e., their inability to care for the aged. But to suggest that there is a parallel here which justifies the way we treat old people in our culture is to assume that the attitudes motivating the behavior are the same. But this seems to be a terrible slur on the Eskimo.

Bibliography

Those interested in pursuing the main theme of this book regarding the nature of virtue, the power of faith, and the mission of the church will find the following books helpful.

Baum, Gregory—*Man Becoming*
   Herder & Herder, New York, 1970.
Evely, Louis—*If the Church is to Survive . . .*
   Doubleday, New York, 1972.
Illich, Ivan—*Celebration of Awareness*
   Doubleday, Anchor, New York, 1971.
Murdoch, Iris—*The Sovereignty of Good*
   Schocken Books, New York, 1971.
Niebuhr, H. Richard—*Christ and Culture*
   Harper Torchbook, TB-3, 1956.
Padovano, Anthony T.—*Dawn Without Darkness*
   Paulist Press, Paramus, New Jersey, 1971.
   —*Free to Be Faithful*
   Paulist Press, Paramus, New Jersey, 1972.
Taylor, Richard—*Good and Evil*
   Collier-Macmillan, London, 1970.
Watts, Alan—*Behold the Spirit*
   Random House—Vintage Book V-761, New York, 1971.
Westley, Richard—*I Believe—You Believe*
   Life in Christ Publ., Chicago, 1972.

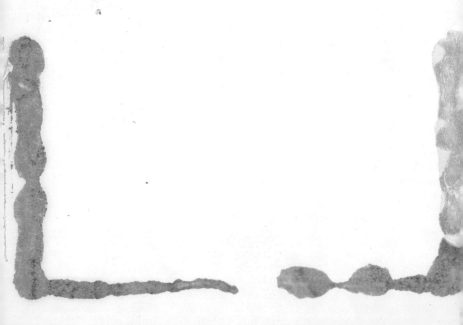